Kiddiwalks

*Thirty short Family Rambles
in and near
West Yorkshire*

*Compiled by members of
The Ramblers' Association
(West Riding Area)*

70th JUBILEE EDITION

Other publications by the Ramblers' Association (West Riding Area)

Douglas Cossar, *Ramblers' Leeds, vol.1 East of Leeds*
Douglas Cossar, *Ramblers' Leeds, vol.2 West of Leeds*
Douglas Cossar, *Ramblers' Bradford*
Douglas Cossar, *Ramblers' Wakefield*
Douglas Cossar, The Airedale Way
Douglas Cossar & John Lieberg, *Country Walks in Mirfield, Emley, Thornhill and Denby Dale*
Douglas Cossar, *The Wakefield Way*
Marje Wilson, *The Brontë Way*
Dales Way Handbook (with the Dales Way Association, annually)

Kiddiwalks first published 1975
50th Jubilee revised edition 1985
60th Jubilee revised and enlarged edition 1995
70th Jubilee completely revised edition 2005

© Ramblers' Association 2005

RAMBLERS' ASSOCIATION (WEST RIDING AREA)
27 Cookridge Avenue, Leeds LS16 7NA

ISBN 0 900613 88 2

Cover photographs by Carol Cowell; other photographs by Douglas Cossar and Keith Wadd

Printed by Hart & Clough, Cleckheaton

Publishers' Note
At the time of publication all footpaths used in these walks were
designated as public rights of way or permissive footpaths, but it should
be borne in mind that diversion orders may be made from time to time.
Although every care has been taken in the preparation of this guide,
the publishers cannot accept responsibility for those who stray
from the routes described.

CONTENTS

The **Ramblers' Association**, a registered charity, is an organisation dedicated to the preservation and care of the countryside and its network of footpaths, and to helping people to appreciate and enjoy them.

Through its Central Office the Ramblers' Association lobbies and campaigns for more effective legislation to achieve
- the preservation and improvement of the footpath network
- better access to the countryside
- the preservation and enhancement for the benefit of the public of the beauty of the countryside.

Since its formation in 1935 the Ramblers' Association has grown into a powerful campaigning organisation with a membership of over 140,000.

The Association relies on many volunteers working at Area and Local Group level to help achieve these objectives.

The **West Riding Area** is one of the 51 Areas of the Ramblers' Association which cover England, Wales and Scotland. It includes the whole of West Yorkshire and parts of North Yorkshire around Selby, York, Harrogate, Ripon, Skipton and Settle, as well as the southern part of the Yorkshire Dales National Park. The Area has over 4,000 members and is divided into 13 Local Groups. For more information visit our website: www.ramblersyorkshire.org

The **Local Groups** carry out the work of the Ramblers' Association by keeping an eye on the state of footpaths in their area and monitoring proposed closures and diversions.
- They put pressure on their Local Authority to take action to remove obstructions and re-instate footpaths after ploughing.
- They do practical work of footpath clearance and waymarking, and can erect stiles and footbridges.
- Where the Local Authority has set up consultation procedures, e.g. Footpath Forums, the Local Group will normally send a representative.
- Many Local Groups produce their own programme of walks.

Regular walks are a very important part of Ramblers' activities. As well as ensuring that local footpaths are used, they provide healthy recreation and the opportunity to make new friends.

If you use and enjoy the footpath network, please help us to protect it, by joining the Ramblers' Association. For further information contact

The Ramblers' Association, 2nd Floor, Camelford House, 87-90 Albert Embankment, London SE1 7TW (Tel.: 020 7339 8500, Fax.: 020 7339 8501; e-mail: ramblers@london.ramblers.org.uk).
Or visit our website: www.ramblers.org.uk

INTRODUCTION

For many rambling couples, the arrival of a family must mark a temporary interruption of many enjoyable outdoor activities while the demands of a new routine are met. Soon, however, first a pram and later a pushchair can find a number of pleasant strolls on which to take their owners. And when walks take one onto rougher terrain, that magnificent invention - or borrowing from American Indians - the papoose, takes over.

Many a thirty-year-old fellwalker has coped with his (or her) incipient middle-aged spread with the help on the back of thirty pounds of child, who enjoys the elevated view, the chance to pull Daddy's (or Mummy's) hair and ears, and falling asleep on a warm back. It is curious how a sleeping baby weighs at least a stone more than one who is awake, even if he kicks less!

The problem occurs at the toddling stage when, too heavy for even the strongest back for more than a couple of hundred yards, the offspring must walk on his own two feet. Perhaps by then there is another occupant of the well-worn papoose, and Mum has enough to carry with orange juice, nappies - and brandy to revive a perspiring Dad!

It was recognition of this problem that encouraged some members of the West Riding Area of the Ramblers' Association - many of whom were also parents of young children - to organise a series of *Kiddiwalks*. A *Kiddiwalk* is a short circular walk (usually anything between 1½ and 4 miles), easy enough for tiny feet to manage, and with enough interest, be it a stream to paddle in, rocks to clamber on, ducks or donkeys, swings or a chute, to catch young imaginations and provide something of the stimulus and experience which is a fundamental reason for taking children out into the countryside. A walk with an interested three- or four-year-old is a linguistic opportunity to be cherished by parent and child alike.

These *Kiddiwalks* proved highly popular, and it was decided to publish some of the best of them in book form. That was thirty years ago, and the demand has proved insatiable. This fully revised edition contains some of the old favourites but also a number of new walks, which we hope will prove equally popular.

We have included walks from each of the five Districts of West Yorkshire and the southern fringes of the Dales. Where possible, details of public transport have been included, but as these change so quickly they should always be checked in advance. The sketch maps which accompany each walk are of course greatly simplified and should not be used as a substitute for the walk description. They are based on the Ordnance Survey's Explorer maps, details of which are given for each walk, and are reproduced by permission of the Ordnance Survey on behalf of H.M.S.O. © Crown copyright 2005. All rights reserved. Ordnance Survey Licence number 100033886.

Remember too that in the Yorkshire climate you need to be suitably dressed and shod for walking. All paths are likely to be muddy in winter and after a spell of rain, and nothing spoils the pleasure of walking so much as being cold and wet.

The walks demonstrate the great variety of West Yorkshire and will provide many talking points for children. As well as the countryside, with its stone walls and stiles, its moorland, pastures, reservoirs, woods and becks, here are an Iron age hill fort, a ruined mediaeval castle, a historic Pennine village with its typical vernacular architecture, a World Heritage Site important in our industrial heritage, three former stately homes with their parks, lakes and gardens, a canal and two steam railways, an RSPB reserve, the literary associations of the Brontës, a wind-farm and exotic animals and butterflies and much more besides.

We hope that this little volume will show parents that they need not be banished from the footpaths, but can share their enjoyment of the countryside with their children from the very beginning, thus starting what is likely to be a lifelong love affair.

This revised edition has been edited by Douglas Cossar with help from John Lieberg and Keith Wadd.

May 2005

This carving can be seen on a house in Heptonstall (Walk 22)

1.   Roundhay Park and Gorge

3 miles (5 km) (full walk), 2¼ miles (3¾ km) (shorter walk). Explorer 289. Leeds is richly endowed with parks and open spaces, and Roundhay is one of the jewels in its crown. Thomas Nicholson, a London banker, bought the 773 acre estate in 1804 and built the Mansion, Leeds's grandest Late Georgian house, in 1826. The estate was bought by the city in 1871 and with its woods and lakes and grassy slopes has been a major recreational resource ever since. The Canal and Coronation Gardens are among the loveliest in the city, and Tropical World, with its collection of exotic plants, animals and butterflies, is now an important tourist attraction (open in summer 10-6, in winter 10-4; admission charge). There are many tarmac paths in the Park, suitable for pushchairs, but the walks described here are not.

By bus: _No.12 Middleton Circular is a frequent service from Leeds Corn Exchange. Alight at Roundhay Park Gates on Prince's Avenue._
By car: _Park at the old tram terminus (the posts which used to carry the overhead wires still survive), now a large car park, off Prince's Avenue at Roundhay Park. Walk back to the main road and turn right - you may like to walk through the sunken rose garden on the right – and cross at the pedestrian crossing._

Worth exploring on this side of the main road are the Canal Gardens, with an entrance close to the bus stop, and further along the Coronation Gardens with Tropical World. Do walk through to the back of these gardens, to where the fountain is. Just to the right of the entrance to Tropical World notice the large fish tank. Here too is the Leeds Millennium Bell, rung every day at noon. Nearby is the Tropical World Café and there are also toilets.

Return to the main road, cross at the pedestrian lights and turn right, crossing the end of Mansion Lane and passing the Roundhay Fox pub. Go through the park entrance ahead of you and follow the tarmac path. At the ornamental shelter keep straight on, noticing to the left the stables of the old mansion, walk through the circular garden and out the other side. Turn left at the T-junction. As you walk along you can see through the trees to the right the arena, where large outdoor events are held. As you approach the Mansion bear right, and turn left at the next major T-junction.

When you reach the next T-junction, cross straight over the road to another ornamental pavilion (there are picnic tables here), but before you reach it bear left over the grass to drop to the path by the Upper Lake. Turn left along the lakeside. There is usually an abundance of bird life on the lake. Towards the end of the lake keep right at a fork, and immediately after crossing a stone bridge fork left on a path which leads through a rather dark wood.

The path emerges by a large gate onto a road. Turn right, but in a few yards fork right up the access road to Roundhay Park Golf Course (municipal) and the Park Lane restaurant. Walk straight through the car park, passing to the left of the clubhouse and restaurant, and through the metal bollards onto a track. In a few yards fork left down a narrower track, and when this peters out, keep straight forward to the hedge in front of you, and walk down with the hedge on your right and the golf course on both sides. When the hedge ends, keep straight on over the fairway (looking out for flying missiles!) to the wood in front, where a clear path leads forward with an old wall and hedge on the right to a gap in the wall ahead.

Walk 1

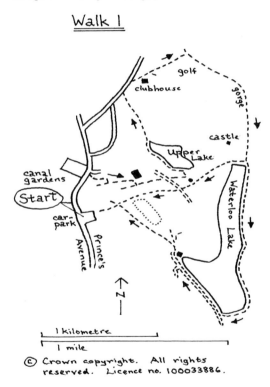

1 kilometre

1 mile

Go through and follow the path, which bears right. The deep valley of Roundhay Gorge is to your left. The path contours some way above the stream. When you reach a cross path (coming from the golf course on the right) turn left downhill to the valley bottom and bear right along the valley path. Count how many times the path crosses the stream! After a time the path climbs again, and now the stream is below you on the right. When you reach a major path junction (the track to the right crosses a stone bridge) keep straight on, soon to reach the large Waterloo Lake (it was built in 1815). Here the routes of the full walk and the shorter walk diverge.

For the **full walk** turn left along the lakeside path and follow it all the way to the dam at the far end. Turn right over the dam, and at the far side bear right again along the tarmac drive. Pass to the left of the large boathouse and walk along with the bollards on your left (there is

8

a car park beyond). Ice cream and refreshments are often available here. Follow the bollards as they bend left over the road, and here there is a small children's playground. Walk clockwise round it, then bear left to a T-junction, where you turn right. Soon you are passing to the left of the arena. When you reach a junction climb the broad steps on the left.

For the **shorter walk** fork right, in a few yards crossing a wooden bridge. Straight ahead over the grass is what looks like a ruined mediaeval castle, but it was built as a ruin in the 19th century. Keep on with the lake to your left, but shortly after the path bends left round the head of the lake, fork right off it up the grass. This is a fine large grassy space for ball games or picnics. Keep up parallel to the wood on your right. At the top of the hill to your right is once again the Upper Lake, but keep ahead over the grass, passing well to the left of the ornamental shelter, cross the tarmac road and keep straight on over the grass. Soon you have the Mansion once more to your right. Pass through a line of trees, cross another tarmac path and keep straight on over more grass, aiming for a broad flight of steps climbing the hillside in front of you. Down to the left is the arena. Drop down to join another tarmac path which leads to the steps.

Now both walks have joined up again. Climb the steps, but shortly before the top fork right by a large curved bench and climb a few more steps. On the left is an area set aside for skateboarding. Then you reach the car park. To reach the bus stop walk straight through the car park to the main road and turn right.

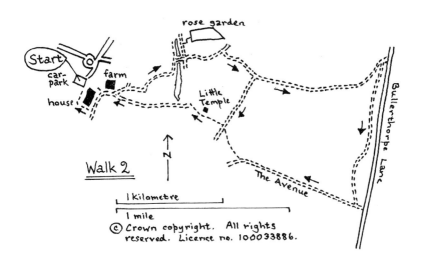

9

2. Temple Newsam

3¼ miles (5¼ km) (full walk), 2 miles (3 km) (shorter walk); both are easy to follow, in a large estate where it is easy to get lost in the woods, but are unsuitable for pushchairs. Many other surfaced paths are available for pushchair users. Explorer 289.

Domesday Book in 1086 records a Manor close to this site as Neuhusum, "New Houses", which became "Newsam". Around 1155 the land became the property of the Knights Templar, hence the "Temple" in the name. The property passed to Thomas Lord Darcy, who built the first large house c.1500-1520. Darcy was beheaded by Henry VIII in 1537 for treason, and his properties were seized by the Crown and given to the King's niece, Margaret, Countess of Lennox. Her son Henry Lord Darnley, the future husband of Mary Queen of Scots, was born here in 1545. In 1622 after a period of neglect Temple Newsam was bought by Sir Arthur Ingram, a London merchant, whose descendants lived here for the next 300 years. He re-modelled most of the Tudor house in the 1620s. The estate was purchased by Leeds Corporation in 1922, and the house is now one of its museums. It has a fine collection of furnishings and paintings. The house is open Tues-Sun in summer 10.30-17.00, in winter 10.30-16.00.

In the 18th-century stable block there are a Visitor Centre (open Tues-Sun in summer 10.00-16.30, in winter 10.00-1530) (pick up a free leaflet here with a plan of the estate), Gift Shop and Café (open in summer Mon-Fri 10.30-17.00, Sat/Sun 10.30-17.30, in winter Tues-Sun 10.30-16.15), and here and near the Walled Garden there are toilets.

The Home Farm nearby (open Tues-Sun in summer 10.00-17.00, in winter 10.00-16.00) in the past provided all the meat, milk and eggs for the family and their servants. Wood from the estate was transformed into doors, gates and fences in the woodyard, and the stonemason, joiner and plumber cared for the house and park from their workshops. The Home Farm is now the largest working Rare Breeds Farm in Europe with over 400 animals. Displays in the original Georgian and Victorian farm buildings bring to life the stories of the past. There are working demonstration days on which you can see traditional crafts in action, and activity sheets and quizzes suitable for the whole family are available in the Visitor Centre.

The estate comprises over 1500 acres of parkland – landscaped by Capability Brown in the 18th-century – woodland and farmland, in which there are many paths and trails. There is a walled garden with a large conservatory and a Rhododendron Walk.

By bus: 63A from Leeds Infirmary Street, half-hourly, Sundays only.
By car: Temple Newsam is 4 miles from Leeds City Centre off the A63 Leeds-Selby road, 2 miles from the M1 Junction 46. There is a car-park close to the house (fee in summer).

The walks start in the courtyard of the house. Stand with your back to the house, looking out over the park. Turn left along the broad tarmac drive. In front of you is the stable block with beyond it the Home Farm. Bear right, leaving both of these on your left. At the first fork after the Farm keep left, and at the next junction keep straight forward (signposted Rose Garden), ignoring a large gate with sphinxes on the left. Walk down the Rhododendron Walk. At the next fork, with the lake straight ahead, keep left (again signposted Rose Garden).

At the next fork bear right over the bridge, then turn left. Pass another bridge on the left, and at the next fork keep right, up to the Rose Garden. At the top of the steps there are toilets on the left, then the entrance to the Aster and Chrysanth Garden, then the entrance to the formal, or Rose Garden. Go in and turn left up to the large conservatory. Walk through the entire length of the glasshouse and leave it by a door on the right at the far end. Turn left to continue your circuit of the formal garden, which you leave by the gate you came in by.

Bear left and walk back down the steps, turning left at the bottom. Pass the bridge you crossed earlier, and at the next fork turn left. Pass between ruined brick buildings and follow the path uphill towards a large gate. Beside this is a strange gate – can you work out how to open it? Pass through (there is a good view back to the conservatory and formal garden) and follow the path up over the field. Pass through another of these curious gates by farm buildings and turn right through a more conventional gate (signposted public footpath Bullerthorpe Lane).

The track bends right and you reach a junction. For the **shorter walk** keep straight ahead here and follow the track until you reach a wood on the right. Here there are kissing gates on both sides: go through the one on the right and climb the path through the wood. It leads to the 18th-century Little Temple, a good viewpoint for the house. Here you rejoin the main walk, so skip the next two paragraphs.

For the **main walk** turn left and follow the track up between hedges. At the top of the hill, where the track bends right and then left, there is a good view back to the house. Pass through another gate and a little further on pass round a metal barrier and bear right, and at the next junction bear right again. Another barrier leads out onto a motor road, but immediately before it turn right along a gravel track (signposted Avenue Woods). An information board tells you that you are walking along beside an earthwork called Grim's Dyke, possibly constructed as a defence for the Celtic kingdom of Elmet, which possibly had a royal centre at Leeds and which was overrun by the Angles in about 617.

After a time the track enters woodland. Follow it until you reach a squeeze stile by a metal gate which gives access to a broad cross track. There is a gate out onto the road to the left, but we turn right along The Avenue, which leads directly to the house in the distance. Walk straight down The Avenue, crossing over the Avenue Ponds in the dip, and at the top of the next rise, where there are benches, fork right off the track and walk down the grass, following the edge of the wood on your right. At the bottom pass through a metal kissing gate, cross over the track to the squeeze stile opposite and follow the path up through the wood. It leads to the 18th-century Little Temple, a good viewpoint for the house, and here you rejoin the shorter walk.

Follow the path past the Temple, in a few yards forking left downhill. At the foot cross the concrete bridge, with the lake to the right, and walk up the track. When you reach the house, bear left and walk past the front of it. Bear right at the end, turn right at the T-junction and in a few yards left to pass along the side of the house. There is a formal garden with box hedges, roses and a fountain on the left. Having passed the house turn right along a paved path, right again, back towards the house, then left to walk along the back of the house, to return to the car-park and bus stop.

Temple Newsam

12

3.   Golden Acre

2½ miles (4 km) (main walk), 1½ miles (2½ km) (shorter walk). Explorer 297. Golden Acre is another of Leeds's parks, situated on the A660 Leeds-Otley road between Adel and Bramhope. It has a large lake, where "feeding the ducks" is the main attraction, gardens, a variety of paths and a café (the Bakery Coffee House, open Mon-Fri 10.30-16.30, Sat/Sun 10.30-17.00). The main walk includes one unprotected crossing of a busy road, leading to a farm where there are usually cattle and horses to be inspected and the former fishpond of Cookridge Hall, a former stately home (now a leisure centre and golf club!). From 1932-38 Golden Acre was an amusement park, and it came to the city in 1945.

By bus: X84 Leeds-Ilkley from Leeds City Bus Station (frequent). From the bus stop walk back towards Leeds for a short distance and turn right into the car-park. Turn immediately left and walk to the far end of the car-park. Arriving from the Ilkley direction, walk on for a short distance and turn left through the main park entrance. Take the first right fork, turn left between the benches and join the walk description at [*].
By car: there is a large car-park on the A660. Walk to the far end away from the entrance.

The walk starts at the far end of the car-park. Go down the steps and bear left through the underpass under the A660. Turn left at the T-junction (if you *only* want to feed the ducks, turn right and follow the path to the lake). The yellow building which soon appears half-right is the café. At a major junction, with several benches on the right, turn right and walk between the benches. [*] Having passed the benches keep left at the fork. Pass the café up on your left, and there is access to it from here. Shortly you reach a short stretch of the former miniature railway which was one of the attractions of the amusement park: it has been planted to give the impression of an abandoned railway line.

Walk along with the old railway down on your right, and at the end of the fence turn right. Pass a small pond on the left and a rock garden on the right to return to the benches you passed a few minutes ago. Pass between the benches once again and turn right up the broad tarmac path. At the T-junction turn left towards the park entrance, but in a few yards turn right up another tarmac drive. When the tarmac turns left through a large gate, keep forward on a track which in a few yards bends left to follow a tall hedge on the left. When the track turns left through another gate, fork right off it on a broad grassy path, which curves right and in a few yards is joined by another path coming from the left.

Follow the broad grassy path forward in the direction of a bare earth path seen ahead. A few yards before you reach this, fork left on a narrower path which soon joins a clear footpath: bear right along this. The park boundary fence is on your left. Soon you pass a large quarry over the wall on your left, and shortly you rejoin the broad path you left a few minutes ago. Bear left through the trees, and then right, with an old wall a short distance off to the left. The path passes an old gate to leave the wood for a large grassy area with heather gardens in the middle. Walk along the left hand edge of the grass, with a wood on the left, for about 60 yards, then turn right to walk across the grass and pass between the various heather gardens.

Walk straight down to the far side of the grass, passing various heather gardens both to the right and to the left, and as you approach the trees at the far side, bear slightly right to pick up a path in the corner back into the wood. Descend this path for a short distance, but at the next junction turn left down a flight of steps. At the foot fork left and join the broad surfaced path over to your left. In a few yards you reach another junction: the surfaced path bears right, there is a kissing-gate on the left, but you keep forward, down towards a stone bridge. Cross the bridge and walk along the embankment of the large lake. Over to the right, on the far side of the lake, you will see the best place for feeding the ducks.

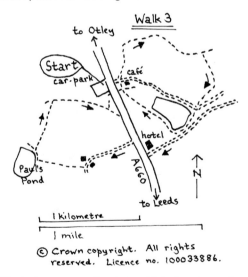

Walk 3

to Otley

Start
car-park

café

hotel

Paul's
Pond

A660

N

to Leeds

1 Kilometre

1 mile

Just after you cross a wooden footbridge you reach a path junction. For the **shorter walk** turn right along the path by the lake. Soon you will reach a sort of jetty with a small building on it sticking out into the lake and an information board illustrating some of the birds you are likely to see on the lake. This is where the main duck-feeding takes place. Continue along the broad path, which will lead you back to the underpass and the car-park.

For the **longer walk** cross the stile on the left and turn right up the track. At the main road turn right along the footway, passing the

Ramada Jarvis Hotel, but cross the road when a suitable gap in the traffic presents itself and continue along the other side. Turn left up the first farm access road. When it forks shortly before Cocker Hill Farm keep left, i.e. straight on, into the farmyard. There is a good likelihood of seeing cattle in the sheds as you pass through. Bear left through the concrete yard, and when the concrete ends, leave the unsurfaced track and go through the gate on the right.

Walk straight over the field, following the old boundary, and soon Paul's Pond appears ahead. On the far side of the field cross the stile and a broad wooden bridge and turn right along the bank of the pond. Shortly before the path turns left at the end of the pond fork right on a path which drops towards the wood. Turn right over the footbridge, but ignore the gate ahead and go through the gap to the left of it and follow the path along the right hand edge of the wood.

After a time you pass through a fence and the path turns right. Keep always on the path closest to the edge of the wood. With the traffic on the A660 a short distance ahead, fork left along a boardwalk. Cross a bridge (the underpass is to your right) and keep forward to return to the car-park. (For buses to Leeds, go through the underpass, turn left and at the T-junction left again to leave the park through the main entrance. The bus stop is to the right.)

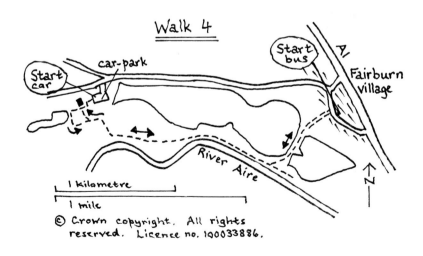

Walk 4

15

Fairburn Ings

4.   Fairburn Ings

3½ miles (5½ km). Explorer 289. Fairburn Ings RSPB Reserve is a 700 acre site beside the River Aire, landscaped on former coal workings. It contains a number of lakes, well provided with hides (don't forget to take binoculars with you!). The boardwalk near the Visitor Centre has a number of information boards aimed at children. The car-park and hides are open daily from 9 a.m. to dusk, the Visitor Centre has more restricted opening hours. At the Visitor Centre are a small shop, toilets and hot and cold refreshments. A Trail Guide is available there. **Note: a circular walk round the reserve is not possible, unless one uses quite a busy road with no footway, so this walk uses the same route both out and back.**

By car: The entrance to the large reserve car-park is on the minor road from Fairburn village to Allerton Bywater (GR 451 278).
By bus: 492 Pontefract-Tadcaster (Mon-Sat daytime hourly) to Fairburn village, the stop near the stump of the market cross.

Route for those arriving by car. From the car-park make your way to the visitor centre. On the way there are picnic tables. From the Visitor Centre follow the sign to Visitor Trails and Hides. At the first T-junction turn right, signposted Pickup Hide, almost immediately turning left again along the fenced boardwalk. At the next fork keep right. The Pickup Hide overlooks a small lake. From the hide go down the steps and at the T-junction turn right. When you reach a junction where the boardwalk goes left, keep straight ahead along the gravel path.

Soon you can make a detour left to the Pond Dipping Platform. Return to the path and continue along it. Ignore another boardwalk on the left and follow the sign to the Riverbank Trail. Pass through a kissing-gate and bear right on a broad track. The path climbs, with a lake down on the right. Turn left through a kissing-gate signposted Riverbank Trail, now on a narrower path. There are glimpses of the River Aire down to the right. After a time the path crosses a concrete drainage pipe and soon swings left at a wooden fence. Further along there are glimpses of the main lake to the left and you pass through another kissing-gate.

In a few yards there is access to a hide on the left overlooking the lake. Return to the path and continue along it. You are now on a high embankment between the lake and the river, a long stretch through light woodland. After a time there is another hide to the left of the path, again overlooking the large lake. Pass through a barrier and emerge from the trees. Fork left away from the river on a broad gravel path. Some way along there is access to the Cut Hide on the right; it overlooks another lake. Return to the path and continue along it.

Follow this path until you reach a point where there is a kissing-gate on the left, a stile on the right and another kissing-gate on the right a few yards further on. This is the furthest point of our walk. If you wish to return by the road, go through the kissing-gate on the left, follow the path across the field to another kissing-gate, then keep ahead along the fenced path to the road and turn left along it. If you wish to visit Fairburn village, keep straight ahead along the track. Otherwise turn round here and follow the same route back.

After you turn left at a large metal gate signposted Visitor Reception and car park and pass through a kissing-gate, look out for a wooden bench on the right. Turn right here along a fenced boardwalk. A few yards before a gate with a no entry sign on it, turn right along a gravel path, which leads back to the Visitor Centre.

Route for those arriving by bus. From the bus stop in Fairburn walk down Gauk Street and turn left down Cut Road, passing Welltrough Cottages. Pass between metal bollards and walk down the track. Go through a metal kissing-gate. There are fine views over the large lake on the right. After a time there is access on the left to the Cut Hide, which overlooks a smaller lake. Return to the path and continue along it. When you reach a grassy area, with the River Aire straight ahead, bear right up some steps and through a wooden barrier.

There now follows a long, elevated walk through light woodland between the river and the large lake. After a time there is a hide on the right of the path, and further along there is access down a path on the right to another hide, both overlooking the large lake. Return to the path and continue along it. In a few yards pass through a wooden kissing-gate and leave the large lake behind. Eventually you pass through another kissing-gate and reach a T-junction, with another small lake straight ahead. Turn right down the track.

Turn left in front of a large metal gate, signposted Visitor Reception and car park, pass through a kissing-gate and just after a wooden bench turn right along a fenced boardwalk. A few yards before a gate with a No Entry sign turn right along a gravel path, which leads to the Visitor Centre.

Return by using the **Route for those arriving by car**, from the Visitor Centre, which is slightly different at the start from your outward route.

5.   Leeds/Bradford Airport and Rawdon Billing

2½ miles (4 km); Explorer 288. An airy walk along pleasant, easy paths with glorious views, culminating in a grandstand view of the main runway at Yeadon Airport.

By bus: No. 97/97A Leeds-Yeadon-Bradford/Guiseley to the junction of Layton Lane/Town Street, Rawdon (on a bend in the main road). Walk along towards Rawdon, enter the churchyard of Rawdon Parish Church on the right and walk towards the church, noticing the old stocks on the left. Just before the church turn right, then go through a gate on the left into a field with a children's playground and the Jubilee Hall beyond. Walk up the tarmac path to the left of the hall and turn left along the next road (Layton Avenue).

By car: Park on Layton Avenue just outside the car-park at the Jubilee Hall, Rawdon, immediately north-east of Rawdon Parish Church (the car-park, although usually empty, is private). There is a children's playground in front of the Hall. With the hall and church to your left walk along Layton Avenue.

At the T-junction turn right along Town Street. Turn right again into the car-park of St.Peter's School and walk up its left hand side, then keep following the high metal fence on your left, with playing fields to your right, to a kissing-gate in the hedge on the far side. Keep straight forward towards the trees on Rawdon Billing, cross a stile by a large metal gate, and walk up the right hand edge of the next field to a gated stile in the wall at the top, then turn left with the wall on your left. When you are faced by a fence straight ahead, ignore the stile in it and turn right uphill.

When you enter the woods, bear left and follow the path round the outside edge of the reclaimed quarry of Rawdon Billing. The views to the left are superb. The path leads to a stile straight ahead into a field. Cross it and keep forward along the top of the slope, after a time ignoring the broad path straight ahead towards a trig point and bearing left to join a fence on the left and follow it down to a stile in it. Cross and walk straight down the next large field, then up the next field to the left hand edge of the hedge at the top.

Either: Keep straight forward up the right hand edge of the next field, but 30 yards before the wall at the far end turn left and walk down the field to a stile by a gate at the bottom. Or: as that path can be very wet, turn left down the track, following it down to the end of the field and turning right along it to the gate. At the gate cross the stile on the left of the track and bear slightly right across the next field towards the houses.

Go through the stile and walk forward to the main road, turn right, and right again at the next traffic lights (Bayton Lane). After about 65 yards fork left along a signposted path and walk diagonally right across the field to a stile in the hedge/fence on the far side (easy to miss!). Bear half left up the next field (this can be wet) to a stile in the fence at the top of a small wood. Bear right to the rather bare top of Plane Tree Hill (can you spot the trig point in the wall?), from where there is a splendid view of the airport. Walk across the hill parallel to the airport on your left to meet a track by the golf course.

Turn right along this to the main road and cross the stile opposite. Cross straight over the enormous field to a gap-stile in the wall on the far side, just to the right of a fenced enclosure and a gate (there is no clear path) and then follow the fence on your right, and where it ends, the old field edge, to a stile at the top of the hill. Now keep forward downhill, still with the line of the old wall to your right, over two more stiles, and at the bottom of the following field go left for a few yards, then right along the edge of the next field to a stile by a gate into a hedged track which leads to a minor road. This is Layton Avenue, and across it is the car park by the Jubilee Hall with the playground.

6.   The Cow and Calf Rocks

2¼ miles (3½ km) by car; 3 miles (5 km) by train/bus; Explorer 297. A moorland walk, visiting an 18th century bath house, a rocky valley, a tarn and some crags popular with climbers; good paths, but a steepish ascent (with many steps) and descent. At the start the walk visits Ilkley's Millennium Green, which has a picnic area and an interesting maze.

By train or bus: There are trains and buses to Ilkley from Leeds, Bradford and Skipton. In addition there are buses from Keighley. From the train/bus terminus walk along the front of the old railway station building towards the town centre, cross the main road on your left at the pedestrian crossing, turn right to cross the foot of Wells Road, then at the telephone kiosk bear slightly left to enter the gardens between the next two streets. Make your way up through the gardens. When you come to a junction, with a bench on the left, fork right and pass underneath a footbridge. At the next junction keep straight ahead uphill, soon keeping right at another fork. The path leads over a footbridge and now the beck is down on your left. Follow the path to the top and turn right up the steps.

*Pass through a little iron gate and walk up to the top of Wells Walk, cross the main road half right into Linnburn Mews, keep forward up the track with the beck still down on your left, and where the track bends right, fork left off it onto a footpath. Cross straight over an access road and follow the path opposite, which leads in a few yards through a kissing-gate. Walk up the path and cross the **second** footbridge on the left, down some steps. Up the other side, the path leads into the car-park. Bear right up some broad steps and turn left to reach the Millennium Maze.*

By car: From the town centre drive up Wells Road. Immediately after crossing the cattle-grid, fork right to the car-park. Walk to the back of the car-park, turn left up some broad steps, then left again to the Millennium Maze.

Try to follow the route through the Maze from one carved stone to the other, then walk down parallel to the road to the car-park, bear right out of it, cross the road at the cattle-grid, turn right into Crossbeck Road, but immediately fork right off it and reach the moor through a small gate. Walk forward up the flight of steps, passing to the left of the paddling pool, and at the top of the steps you will see your first goal, the white house some distance up the hillside. The path leads more or less straight to it, with lots more steps to climb on the way. At White Wells, a bath house built in the 18th century by Squire Middleton for the people of Ilkley, there are benches and picnic tables, and a fine view; sadly there seems at present to be no access to the bath house. Down to the right there are toilets.

The walk continues up the steps to the left of the house, crossing a cross path at the back of it. At the top of the flight of steps you reach a broad cross path: turn left up it. Can you notice the remains of paving on this path, which was one of the old routes across the moor? Shortly after a sharp left hand bend in the path and about 40 yards before you reach the bottom of another long flight of steps, which leads up through the crags, take the path forking left, which leads through the rocks along the base of Ilkley Crags. You pass above the top edge of a narrow wood down on your left and then walk through Rocky Valley. There are remains of paving on this path too.

At the far end of the valley take the left fork, which leads down towards some rocks in the distance. These are the Cow and Calf, our next objective. Ford Backstone Beck and immediately turn left, walking downhill, with the beck to your left for a short distance, but soon you bear right away from it. Notice the clear path forking left, which descends the rim of the valley of Backstone Beck, with the beck down to its left, for that will be our return route. But for the moment keep forward towards the rocks ahead, passing to the right of a deep quarry just before you reach them. There will probably be climbers on the crags. If you want to reach the foot of them, walk round anti-clockwise until you reach the broad descending path. At the foot there is also a kiosk with refreshments. From the top there is a fine view over Wharfedale. Over the roof of the Cow and Calf Hotel you can see Otley Chevin, further left are the Arthington railway viaduct, Almscliff Crag and the mast above the Washburn valley.

To return to Ilkley, set off on the path you came by, passing this time of course to the left of the deep quarry, but instead of following your outward path back up the hill, fork right and continue along the edge of the quarry. Towards the far end fork left, and the path begins to descend, in the direction of the narrow wood you passed on your outward route, and soon you have the deep gorge of Backstone Beck to your left. Keep on the main path as it steepens and leads down to a cross path. Turn left and cross Backstone Beck by the wooden footbridge.

Again keep on the main path, which climbs over a slight rise and then drops to The Tarn. Walk along the right hand bank of the tarn, and at the far end follow the broad track, partly macadamed, down to leave the moor by a large gate just to the right of the small gate you used at the start. Motorists will bear left and cross the cattle-grid to return to their cars, those who came by bus or train will cross over Crossbeck Road and this time walk straight down the hill to the town centre.

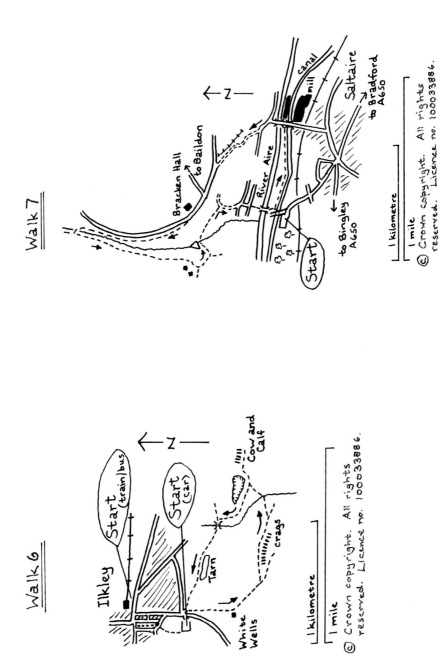

Walk 7

Walk 6

23

7.   Shipley Glen

3½ miles (5½ km); Explorer 288. This walk has it all: a Water Bus on the canal in summer between Hirst Wood and Shipley (information on 01274-595914, Shipley Glen Tramway (open Easter - September and winter Sundays), Glenaire Play Park, with swings, seesaws, etc, a small children's funfair (open every day during the school summer holidays), Bracken Hall Countryside Centre (open 12.00-17.00 May - August except Mon. & Tue, September, October and April Wed, Sat, Sun only, November - March Wed. & Sun. only), the World Heritage Site of Saltaire, the model village built by Bradford millowner Sir Titus Salt on the banks of the River Aire in the middle of the 19th century, which includes Salts Mill, with its David Hockney exhibition, art bookshop and café, and of course a famous beauty spot, with a stream, rocks to clamber on and any number of places for a picnic.

By bus: From Bradford No. 679 runs to Hirst Wood (weekdays hourly); alight at Dallam Avenue/Slenningford Grove and walk down Hirst Lane over the railway bridge, to start the walk at Hirst Wood car park.

By train: Alight at Saltaire station, turn left down the village street, with the mill on the right, cross the canal, and where there is access to the towpath on the left, turn right and pick up the walk description at [*].

By car: Turn down Clarence Road at Saltaire roundabout and continue down Hirst Lane, crossing the railway bridge to Hirst Wood car park on the left. The walk starts here.

Cross the canal bridge (Water Bus stop) and turn right along the towpath of the Leeds and Liverpool Canal. Pass Saltaire playing fields to your left. Turn left off the towpath just before the road bridge crosses the canal at Salts Mill (or visit Saltaire village – information leaflet available - and the Hockney exhibition) and [*] cross the River Aire by a tubular metal bridge signposted 'Shipley Glen ¾, Shipley Glen Tramway'. Carry straight on through Roberts Park to reach Higher Coach Road (Glenaire Play Park is situated immediately across this road). Cross the road and turn left to a public bridleway sign and turn right up the bridleway, passing the Glen Tramway which you can take if you wish. A small exhibition about the Tramway may be open. Otherwise continue uphill through the wood.

On reaching the road follow the sign for Shipley Glen (a small funfair, open during the summer school holidays, can be found on the left). Continue past the Old Glen House pub to reach open moorland on the left and the Glen Tea Rooms. There are toilets here. A little further on along the road is Bracken Hall Countryside Centre. Continue along the rock-strewn plateau with the beck in the valley on your left, following the general direction of the road to your right, for quite a way, until you reach a footpath sign on the left of the road where the wall ends to the right (up on the right you may see model aeroplanes or hang gliders flying).

Bear slightly left away from the road and follow the path between concrete bollards down to the beck. Cross the bridge and follow the track, which is now tarmac, to the next junction, there turning left up Lode Pit Lane. Before you reach the top of the hill fork left on a clear but unmarked path. At first it drops gently – ignore a path forking right uphill - then it contours for a few yards before climbing to a wall.

Contour along, never far from this wall to your right, but high above the beck. As you pass cream-painted bungalows to your right, fork left steeply down to an old dam. Turn left along the dam wall, crossing the beck where it leaves the dam. At the end of the iron fence bear right uphill on a wide path through the wood. On reaching a wall corner on the right, bear right on the level path, ignoring the ascending path ahead. After passing through holly bushes it becomes a walled lane.

At a junction turn right into a descending lane. On reaching the road cross it and continue straight ahead into Bowland Avenue (passing the bus shelter on your left). Cross a minor road and continue to a grey tubular bridge in sight ahead. Cross the river by the bridge and keep ahead to a gap in the wall and up the steps to the canal. Turn right along the towpath, then left over the bridge to return to your starting point.

Coppice Pond, St. Ives

8.   St.Ives

The St. Ives estate is situated off the B6429 Bingley-Harden road. It was originally called Harden Grange, a name which indicates monastic ownership. It was owned by the Knights Templars and the Knights Hospitallers, but in the 13th century it was given to the Cistercian Rievaulx Abbey. After the Dissolution of the Monasteries under Henry VIII it changed hands twice before being bought by Robert Ferrand in 1636; his family owned it until 1928 when it was transferred into public ownership. The Ferrand family were well known in this area from the 1500s, having previously been custodians of Skipton Castle. Since 1929 it has been the headquarters of the Sports Turf Research Institute (STRI), an advisory service to golf clubs; in 1931 a 9-hole golf course was laid out, extended to 18 holes in 1935. The main house, which is largely of 19th-century date, is now a private nursing home.

There are three signposted trails through the estate, a green one of 1 kilometre, with green discs depicting a hedgehog, a blue walk of 2¼ kilometres, with blue discs showing a frog and a red walk of 7 kilometres, with red discs portraying a squirrel. Our two walks use parts of all of these. The longer walk is of 2¾ miles (4½ km), the shorter one is of 1¾ miles (2¾ km). Of the two, the shorter walk is slightly more strenuous, having more ups and downs, the longer one is just about suitable for pushchairs. Explorer 288.

By bus: 616 Bradford-Bingley (half-hourly), 727/729 Keighley-Bingley-Wilsden/Cullingworth (hourly) and walk up the access road for ½ mile until you reach on the right a car-park, toilet block and large children's playground.
By car: The entrance to St. Ives is signposted from the B6429 road. Drive up the access road for ½ mile until you reach on the right a car-park, toilet block and large children's playground. Park here.

Longer walk. From the car-park take the broad tarmac road signposted to Bingley St. Ives Golf Club and the STRI. There is a good view of the mansion. At the next junction turn left, with the golf course on your right. Pass the clubhouse and some garages on the right, an interesting older building on the left, then the former stables and coachhouse and the Home Farm on the right. Another older building is passed on the right, and on the left a gap in the wall gives access to picnic tables. The road now passes between high walls and through a gateway.

Continue along the road, ignoring a track coming in from the left, but fork right off it past a large gate. Climb a few steps on the right to the bank of the Coppice Pond and turn left, soon rejoining the main path. Follow this along, with the lake on the right. At the end of the lake keep straight on through a gateway. Pass a junction where the blue route comes in from the left and keep always to the main path, which after a time begins to climb. Look out for a flight of steps on the left which lead to Lady Blantyre's Rock. A memorial tablet explains its significance. Then return to the main path and continue up it.

Soon you have heather moorland on the left and a high wall on the right, and further on in two places you have the golf course on both sides. Keep on until a metal kissing-gate leads out of the St. Ives estate. Turn right along the track and enjoy fine views to the left over Airedale. Pass round a large gate and reach a track junction, with a gateway back into St. Ives on the right. That is our onward route, but it is worth making a short detour to the Druid's Altar, a well-known viewpoint.

So follow the signpost pointing left past a large wooden gate. A narrow, often muddy path through the bracken and heather leads in about three minutes to the edge of the escarpment and a massive rock projecting into the void. This is the Druid's Altar. Don't try to climb on to it, but enjoy the superb views from the edge. Then retrace your steps and re-enter the St. Ives estate.

In a few yards keep left on the

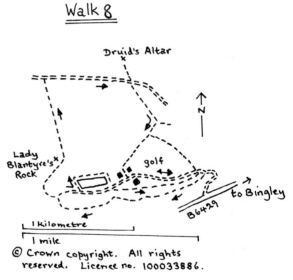

Walk 8

broad walled track. At a stone barn on the left of the track keep right at the fork on the main track. Soon there is a view left down to Bingley. At the next junction keep straight on, ignoring Blind Lane to the left. Pass round a gate and keep forward at the junction. Follow the track down to a large car-park, bear left and pass between the clubhouse and the home farm. At the T-junction turn left, and at the next junction turn right to return to your starting point.

Shorter walk. From the car-park walk back down the access drive. Look out for a signposted path pointing right: you pass round a large gate and are immediately faced by a fork. Keep left on the descending path. At a junction with a derelict stone barn ahead turn right. After a time a sunken overgrown area on the right indicates a former pond. The path climbs gently, passes behind a house on the left and starts to descend again. On the right a waterfall comes tumbling down the hillside. Pass through a kissing-gate and turn sharp right, with a high wall on your right.

The path is now climbing again and the wall soon ends. At the next junction fork left, following the blue (frog) walk. Cross some rocks which are provided with a handrail. Some way further along ignore a footpath sign pointing left to Cuckoo Nest. Keep forward, in a few yards joining a tarmac road. Cross straight over and follow the path opposite, which climbs some steps. At the next junction turn right. When you reach the Coppice Pond, turn left, with a wall on your left and the lake to your right. Follow the lakeside path the entire length of the lake. Near the far end you pass archery butts on the left.

Bear right round the top end of the lake and start walking back down the other side, but after a short distance drop down some steps on the left and turn left to pass round a large gate out onto a tarmac road. Turn left along it. Pass between high walls. Opposite an old house on the left go through a gap in the wall on the right and follow the grit path as it winds down to some picnic tables. Leaving these on your left, follow the grit path towards the wood, pass between two old stone gateposts and turn sharp left. To the right here is a tunnel under the road you have just walked along.

In a few yards at the junction bear left. A little further on ignore a path forking right and a few yards after that keep left at what looks like a fork, to follow a wooden fence on the left. From this path you soon have a good view of the Victorian mansion. At the next fork keep left, with a mossy wall on your left. For a few yards there is a wall on both sides. Then bear slightly left through the trees to return to the car-park.

9.   Haworth and the Worth Valley Railway

3 miles (5 km); Explorer OL21. Tourists come to Haworth mainly for two reasons, the Brontë family connections – the parsonage where they lived is now a museum, open daily April-September 10-5.30, October-March 11-5, closed in January - and the steam trains of the Keighley and Worth Valley Railway. This railway was the setting of the film of E.Nesbit's *The Railway Children*, and our walk coincides with part of the 5-mile "Railway Children Walk", described in an attractive leaflet available from the Haworth Tourist Information Centre (30p). The walk starts at Haworth Railway Station, where there is a railway museum and a well equipped bookstall.

By train: Trains from Leeds, Bradford and Skipton to Keighley, there changing onto the Keighley & Worth Valley Railway. There are steam trains every day in summer and at weekends in winter.
By car: Park in Haworth and walk down to Haworth Station, using the last paragraph of the walk description from the village centre.

On emerging from the station turn right along the main road. When it bends sharp right at the War Memorial fork left along Brow Road, which in a few yards bends left. Opposite you will see a footpath signposted to Oxenhope. Climb the steps and follow the flagged path by a high wall. The clear path leads up the valley of Bridgehouse Beck, with good views of the railway.

Follow the path through several fields and kissing-gates. It crosses a footbridge over a deep channel. Pass through some metal bollards. In the next field ignore a path forking right, and keep straight forward, soon with a fence to your right. Pass to the right of a derelict cottage and reach a stile in the wall corner ahead. Follow the fence/wall on your right, and bear right along a track in front of a house called Ives Bottom.

At the far end of the garden pass through a gate and immediately turn right down the remains of an old walled lane. Admire but do not cross the packhorse bridge, and keep along by the beck, crossing a stile, to reach another stile in a stone wall. Pass through and shortly cross the beck by a tubular bridge. Follow the wall on your left to the next stile – there is a farm to the right – and continue along the farm road. It leads past a sewage treatment works! Where the road bends left to cross the beck keep forward through a kissing-gate with the beck still on your left, soon entering another old walled lane.

Opposite a footbridge over the beck on the left cross the step-stile on the right, bear sharp right and then left over the railway (care!) – Oxenhope Station is a short way along to the left - then left up to a stile on the right, then steeply up the slope with a wall to the left. The house at the top of the slope over this wall is Bents Farm, otherwise known as Three Chimneys, the home of the Railway Children. Follow the wall round to the right of the house, go through the stile by the gate and turn left to the front of the house.

Straight ahead through a gap-stile is a path to Oxenhope Station, from where you could take the train back to Haworth or Keighley. Follow it past some bungalows and into a road; turn left down the hill to the station.

But our walk turns right up the access road, left at the next motor road, then right up Old Oxenhope Lane. Where the road bends left at Old Oxenhope Farm turn right into the farmyard then immediately left past a large stone trough to follow the wall on your left up to a stile by a large gate. Keep on by the wall on your left, soon entering a narrow walled lane by a gap-stile (don't miss it!). Where this ends the wall is now on your right. Cross a stile and a walled lane, and keep on by the wall on your right. The path drops towards some renovated houses. Pass to the left of these and bear left up the access road, but where this bends left keep straight ahead through a gated stile.

Walk straight across the field, soon with a wall to your right. When your way ahead is blocked by a wall turn right down a walled path. Follow this as it bends left, then right, then left again, and now keep forward all the way back to Haworth. The path leads past the churchyard, with the Parsonage Museum up to the left, and the church, to reach the main street.

Walk down the cobbled street with its numerous gift shops and cafés. About halfway down, opposite the Fleece, fork left down a steep cobbled lane (signposted Railway Station), cross the main road at the bottom and either continue straight down Butt Lane (turning left at the bottom to cross the railway by a footbridge), or, more attractively, fork right into the park. Head downhill, and when you reach a broad tarmac drive with benches, turn right for a few yards then left down some steps. At a circular tarmac space with bushes in the middle keep straight on. Cross over the basketball pitch – there is a children's playground along to the right – and continue down some steps and a narrow tarmac path with high bushes to the left. This leads to a long flight of steps, then out onto a road. Turn left, pass the end of the cobbled Butt Lane and cross the railway by the footbridge to the station.

Walk 10

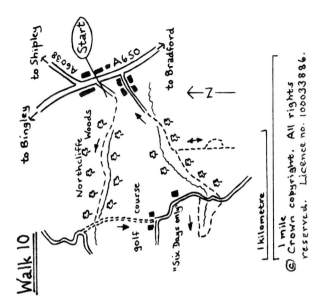

Walk 9

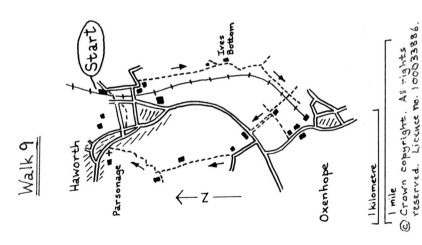

10. Northcliffe Woods, 'Six Days only' and Heaton Woods

3.3 miles (5.3 km); Explorer 288. Woodland paths, a miniature railway on which one can have rides (open most Sunday afternoons from March to September), a small recreation ground (swings, shute, climbing frame).

By bus: No. 622/623 (Scholes-Bradford-Bingley-Eldwick, Mon-Sat); 626 (Brighouse-Bradford-Shipley-Baildon, Mon-Sat); 651 (Bradford-Airport Circular, Mon-Sat); 653 (Bradford-Otley-Harrogate); 97 (Bradford-Leeds, daily); 662 (Bradford-Bingley-Keighley, daily). Alight at attractive gardens forming the grounds of some blocks of flats about 250 yards on the Bradford side of the junction of the A650 (to Bingley) and the A6038 (to Otley), opposite Norwood Terrace, and walk along Cliffe Wood Avenue.

By car: About 250 yards on the Bradford side of the junction of the A650 (to Bingley) and the A6038 (to Otley) turn into Cliffe Wood Avenue and drive along to the car park.

Walk along to the end of the car park and enter the woods on the wide valley track. Where the tarmac track narrows there is the miniature railway on the left. Continue up the valley path, past picnic tables, soon with a beck on the left, for quite a distance. Where the path forks, take the left fork leading across the beck and up some steps. At the top of the slope, keep ahead on the path between two parts of Northcliffe golf course (still wooded). Keep ahead through a gap-stile into an enclosed path.

At the motor road turn left (take care, because there are blind bends and no footway) and follow the road round to a group of 17th-century houses - officially 'Heaton Royds' but always known locally as 'Six Days Only'. Just before the cottages there is a horse trough on the right inscribed 'J.Field Esquire'. As the road drops steeply take a signposted path on the right leading into the wood high above the beck, Weather Royds Wood. Turn left across the head of the gill, and left again at two old gateposts (ignoring the path descending left by steps into the valley) to follow the track with the beck now down on your left and soon a wall on the right. Reach the next road by a gap-stile beside a gate, cross it diagonally right and enter Heaton Woods through another stile.

After a time a better path comes in from the right: keep straight on along it. Look out for and take a narrow ascending path forking right, and where it levels out ignore a minor path forking right through a broken wall. Where the wall on the right ends, just before a gap-stile ahead, a steep path leads up to the right. Climb Cat Steps, with a fine view back over Airedale (Can you spot the radio masts on Ilkley Moor?).

At the top keep forward along the track to reach Heaton Hill Recreation Ground on the right, entered through a gap in the wall. This pleasant grassy area would be a suitable place for a picnic. On leaving it through the same wall gap, turn right along the cobbled lane for 20 yards, turn left on a tarmac path between the houses, then left at the next street. At the end of this, with St Barnabas Primary School on the right, keep ahead on the track between hedges, bearing left when this forks. At the next cross track turn right to rejoin the top of Cat Steps.

Walk back down these and keep straight on down. Ignore a stile in the wall on the right. Keep always down the main path, not far from the wall on the right. When you reach a clear cross path, bear right and pass to the left of a wooden kissing-gate on a path which soon descends by a few steps. About 20 yards after these turn sharp left on a path which soon descends to the beck by more steps.

Turn right and follow the beck, crossing it by a wooden footbridge at Rocky Crossing. From the bridge bear right for 15 yards, then fork half-left away from the beck on a gently rising path. Keep right at the next T-junction. The path keeps parallel to the beck and leaves the woods through a barrier. Follow the dirt track to the right of houses. At the tarmac road keep forward, and at the main road turn left to return to the starting point.

Walton Hall (Walk 11)

11. Anglers Country Park and the Heronry

Explorer 278. Anglers Country Park, near Wintersett, was opened in 1986 on the site of a reclaimed opencast coal mine. It has a large lake, and with the surrounding woods and reservoirs it forms a haven for birds and wild flowers. The Waterton Countryside Discovery Centre (variable opening hours) has displays and toilets. A free informative leaflet on the area is published by the Wakefield Countryside Service. Squire's Tearoom is open in the summer every day 10-5. The 2 mile walk round the lake is suitable for pushchairs.

Charles Waterton (the "Squire") (1782-1865) lived at Walton Hall (built in 1767 and now part of the Waterton Park Hotel), where his family had lived since 1453. After travels in Guyana and Brazil he returned home in 1820 and dedicated his life to observing and protecting the local wildlife, creating what is what is said to be the world's first nature reserve.

The Barnsley Canal was opened in 1799 to carry coal from Barnsley and grain from Wakefield. Waterton's father refused to allow the canal to go through the park. Instead, large cuttings had to be hewn out of the rock to the west of the estate. Subsidence and the railway era caused its decline. It is now a Site of Scientific Interest and home to frogs, water plants and several species of dragonfly.

The Heronry is 350 hectares of open countryside which includes the former Walton Hall Estate, Anglers Country Park, two more reservoirs built to supply water to the canal, woodland and farmland.

Our suggested walk, which takes in part of the Walton Hall Estate and some of he woodland, is 3½ miles (5½ km) long. The route is waymarked almost throughout with red Waterton Trail waymarks.

By bus: 195, 196 (Wakefield to Newstead/S.Hiendley/Hemsworth) to Wintersett; continue through the village, and after leaving it take the first minor road on the right, signposted to Anglers Country Park, and follow it to the main car park.
By car: Anglers Country Park is west of Wintersett village and is signposted from the A638 at Crofton and the A61 at Notton; park in the main car park by the visitor centre (GR 375 153).

From the Countryside Centre take the main track heading towards the lake, soon with a hedge/fence on your left. Shortly before you reach the lake, keep left at the fork. Soon you have the lake on your right for a short distance. Just before the track bends right there is access on the left to the hide overlooking the pond in the nature reserve. At the next fork keep left, ignoring the track which passes the large gate on the right. About 180 yards further along cross a stile on the left and a few yards further on another stile.

Follow the fence on the right along, with the golf course ahead. Cross a stile by a gate and continue by the hedge/fence on the right. At the bottom of the field cross the stile, footbridge and stile and bear slightly right across the large field. On reaching the remains of the high Walton Hall estate wall (built in 1824 to keep poachers out and wildlife in) cross the first stile and immediately turn sharply back left, to walk back along the inside of the wall, with the golf course on your right. Just after passing some small ponds on the right, at the entrance to Stubbs Wood, bear slightly right on the main path. At a

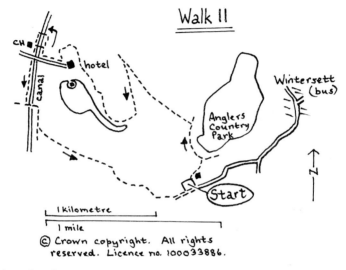

Walk 11

crossing of paths some way into the wood keep straight on.

After a time you have the lake on your left. On leaving the wood you join a track coming from the golf course on your right; a little further on keep straight on at the junction. To the left, in the lake, is the Waterton Park Hotel. When the track bends left, fork right off it, up three steps and along a path with a small wood on the left. At the end of the wood turn left down the edge of the wood to rejoin the track. Cross it diagonally right onto a grassy footpath. The large modern building down on your left is part of the hotel.

Cross a grassy track coming up from the hotel. Look out for a fork, where you keep left on a footpath which drops to the left of a corrugated metal tank to reach another cross track. Turn left and cross a shallow valley. At the end of the fence on your left fork left off the track, passing to the right of a holly bush and bearing right uphill over rough ground.

The path leads up to a doorway in a red brick wall. Go through and turn left. Follow the path to a road, but turn right up the grass just before it. Cross straight over a track into the golf course by a green metal barrier, and when you are faced by a wall, turn right. Over the wall is the disused Barnsley Canal. This is the same high wall as the one we met at the bottom of the estate. Ignore the golfers' footbridge, leading to the clubhouse, and keep on until you reach a doorway in the wall: go through, cross the canal, hardly recognisable here, and turn left.

An information board gives you more background on the Trans-Pennine Trail and the Canal. Just after it notice the overgrown remains of a lock. Pass the golfers' footbridge again, walk under a bridge and follow the towpath until you reach a path forking right slightly uphill. Go up, pass through a small wood and turn left along the track, to cross the canal and turn right.

When the high wall on the left bends left, stay with it and follow it through the wood, but where it bends sharp left, bear slightly right with the track (there is a gate in the corner of the wall here). At a major fork near the end of the wood keep left, soon passing through a stile by a large metal gate. When the tarmac road begins, follow it back to the start of the walk.

Walk 12

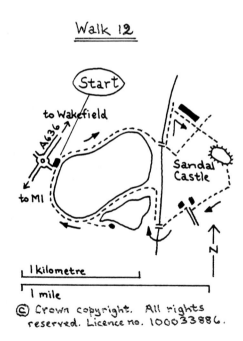

36

12. Pugneys Country Park and Sandal Castle

2¾ miles (4½ km); Explorer 278. Lots to explore. Pugneys Country Park is situated on the A636 Wakefield to Denby Dale road, about a mile from the M1 Exit 39. The entrance is from a roundabout and it is well signposted. The Park is run by Wakefield Leisure Services. Canoes, pedaloes, sailing dinghies and windsurfers can be hired, and an electric launch carrying eight people can be hired for a 30 minute trip round the lake. A miniature railway offers train rides at weekends and on Bank and school holidays (weekends and Bank holidays from 11.00, other running days from 13.00). There are two hides to cater for birdwatchers. A gravel path suitable for pushchairs leads round the main lake, a walk of 1½ miles. There are toilets near the entrance.

The name Pugneys, or Pugnals, dates back to mediaeval times and means "goblins' nook", a mystical dwelling. In these times the wet conditions led to the establishment of osier reed beds, which were used for basket making. The landscape was drastically altered in the 1900s, when the site was excavated for sand and gravel. The Coal Board acquired the site for open-cast mining 1972-79. The Country Park opened 1st August 1985. It extends to 250 acres, including a 75 acre water sports lake and a 20 acre nature lake.

The first Sandal Castle was built by William de Warenne soon after 1106. He was the son of one of the noblemen who came to England from Normandy with William the Conqueror. He owned the Manor of Wakefield. He needed both a home and a place to defend himself when he came to Wakefield. His family owned the castle almost continuously for another 240 years. Later the castle came into the ownership of the Crown and the buildings were neglected. The castle was further damaged during a siege in the Civil War in 1645, and in the following year it was demolished. The Visitor Centre, with toilets and refreshments, is open in summer every day 11.00-16.30, in winter at weekends 12.00-16.00.

By bus: The 443/444 Leeds-Wakefield-Hall Green bus (every 15 minutes Mon-Sat daytime, hourly evenings and Sun) will drop you near the roundabout.
By car: Car park in the Country Park.

From the car park walk left round the lake. There are picnic tables near the start. You can use the path or the grass. Follow the gravel path round the end of the lake, passing between a young wood on the left and a prominent red lifebuoy by the water's edge, and at the far end of the wood look left to see a footbridge pointing towards the castle. Cross it and turn left along the drain. Notice the bulrushes and Himalayan balsam growing in the water. Turn right before the redbrick flats and keep them on your left. Where the houses end cross over a cross track and keep forward towards the castle.

As you approach the far side of the field bear right and enter the castle grounds through a gap in the hedge. Climb the grass bank. There are several information boards within the castle site. Cross the bridge over the moat and climb the steps to the highest point. At the top enjoy the magnificent view. Can you spot Wakefield Cathedral, the Town Hall and St.John's Church? Work your way round, look over the lake and find the car park from which you started. This lake is solely for water sports, whilst the smaller one on the left is a nature reserve. Can you see the Emley TV mast and the windfarm near Penistone? Go down the steps again and explore the castle.

Cross back over the moat and turn right on the gravel path, keeping within the castle grounds. When the path curves right at the far end of the ruins, take a path on the left by a bench slanting down to a redundant stile, then keep forward with the fence to your left. When this fence turns left uphill, keep forward to the facing fence and turn right downhill beside it. At the road turn right, then left in front of the old farm buildings. Keep straight ahead, cross the bridge over the drain and bear right along the wire fence. When the grass becomes greener (this may sound odd, but it's very clear when you get there!), turn left.

At the lake turn left again. After a time you reach a bench and a hide overlooking the smaller lake. A good distance further along a broad track forking back left leads to the other hide. From it retrace your steps and continue round the main lake, walking near the edge if you wish, soon passing the miniature railway. It is not far now to your starting point.

Sandal Castle

13. The Yorkshire Sculpture Park

The Yorkshire Sculpture Park contains a fascinating outdoor exhibition of sculpture set in the parkland of an 18th/19th-century stately home, Bretton Hall, which is now part of the University of Leeds. There is a great deal to see, so give yourselves plenty of time. There are toilets, a shop, a coffee bar, café and restaurant in the new Visitor Centre, where the walk starts. Whether you start from the Visitor Centre or the Information Kiosk, be sure to pick up a free Map Guide, which has among other things several suggested walking routes through the Park, and if you are particularly interested in Henry Moore, a plan of his sculptures in the Old Deer Park.

Our walk, through some of the parkland, with a chance to visit a selection of the sculptures and admire the wildfowl on the lakes, is of 2½ miles (4 km); Explorer 278.

By bus: The X41 (Leeds University–Leeds City Square–Wakefield–Bretton College–Barnsley, 446/447/448 Leeds-Wakefield-Barnsley/Denby Dale will take you to the Information Kiosk in the Sculpture Park. The X41 is more frequent in the university terms than in the vacations. Start the walk at [*].
By car, leave the M1 at Junction 38 and follow the A637 in the direction of Huddersfield; the entrance into the Yorkshire Sculpture Park is signposted after a mile at a new roundabout. Follow the access road to the new Visitor Centre (pay and display car-park).

Our walk, starting at the Visitor Centre, sets off through the Old Deer Park, where a number of sculptures by Henry Moore are exhibited, crosses the River Dearne and heads out into the countryside to the south of the Park, before returning for a walk through the Sculpture Park itself.

On leaving the new Visitor Centre by the main entrance turn right, then right again, pass a door into the coffee bar, go down a few steps, turn left through a gate and walk along parallel to the car-park with a fence on your left. The path bears right away from the fence down to Henry Moore's *Reclining Mother and Child*. Keep the same direction down across the grass, crossing a track leading to Bretton Chapel of 1744 on the left, pass to the right of another Moore sculpture, the *Three Piece Reclining Figure No.1* and continue down the hill, crossing a track at a gateway (if the gate is locked there is a stile a little lower down the fence) and on to the *Two Piece Reclining Figure No.1*. Canada geese have made quite a mess of the grass in several places in the Park. Now continue to a charming 18th-century bridge. Go through the iron gate and cross the bridge and the dam which follows.

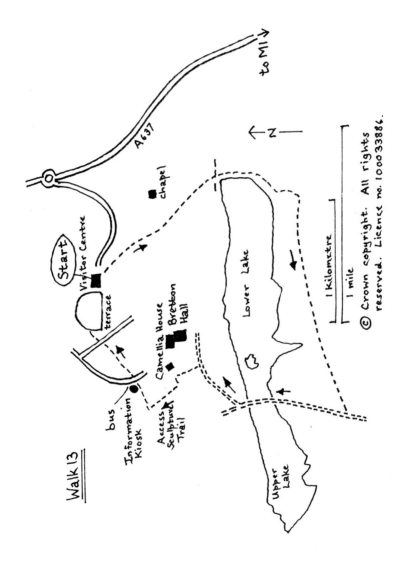

Walk 13

Start

Visitor Centre

terrace

bus

Information Kiosk

Access

Sculpture Trail

Camellia House

Bretton Hall

chapel

A637

to M1

Lower Lake

Upper Lake

N

1 Kilometre

1 mile

On the far side bear right with the track, to pick up a stone wall on the left. This leads round to a well, built, as the inscription tells you, by Grace, Countess of Eglinton in 1685. Continue along the track with the lake to your right, as far as the gate into the conservation area, where you must bear left up the steps up the hillside. The path leads through woodland, then at the end of the wood it descends a few steps and climbs to a stile. Go through the stile and follow the path in the direction of the Emley Moor mast. There is a fine view over the lake to the Hall.

Eventually you pass through an old hedge of tall trees and bear left off the track. The rising path crosses a large field. Cross a stile in the fence and continue your line up the next pasture towards the stile on the far side, but instead of crossing the stile turn right down the track with the

"...where you must bear left up the steps up the hillside..."

fence to your left. There is a fine view of the Hall. Walk straight on through the iron gate by the ornamental gateposts, and cross two bridges (look out for wildfowl), then bear right to a stile and kissing-gate into the Yorkshire Sculpture Park.

Now follow the broad track forward in the direction of the Hall. Where this track bears right to pass in front of the Hall turn left off it over the grass through the trees (no path) to pass to the right of the cricket pavilion and a dense rhododendron hedge. When you reach the fine

Camellia House (c.1817) to your right (it may be open if you would like to look inside) and the old tennis courts (now a car park) ahead, bear left to the "Bird Cage", a piece of iron trellis work once overlaid

The Camellia House with large hare on anvil point

with netting and used as an aviary, where you enter the Access Sculpture Trail.

Totem pole in the Access Sculpture Trail

This award-winning trail, designed for easy wheelchair access, was laid out mainly between 1985 and 1990. Explore it slowly to enjoy its great variety of sculptures, plants and landscape effects. Walk through the Bird Cage and out the other side, and follow the path through the rhododendrons. In a few yards fork left and a few yards further on turn right, to walk along the "Brick Tunnel". Immediately after this turn left (contrary to the direction of the arrows on the ground) to emerge into a lovely landscaped area. Make your way up to the far end of the Trail, which you leave through a pergola into a car park. Walk forward across the car park, bearing left past the Kennel Block (in which there are toilets) to reach on the left the Information Kiosk.

[*] Leaving the car parks on the right cross straight over the tarmac drive and climb the grassy hillside, passing through Barbara Hepworth's *Family of Man*. At the top cross over another tarmac drive and continue over the grass to a gap in the tall yew hedge over to your right into the Bothy Garden. This gives access to the Pavilion Gallery and the Bothy Shop and Gallery (with toilets). At the far end is the back entrance to the new Visitor Centre. Just before you reach it another gap in the hedge on the right gives access to the Formal Terrace and Formal Garden. Pass through the Visitor Centre. Those who came by bus should now go to the start of the walk description.

14. Hemsworth Water Park and Vale Head Park

Hemsworth Water Park is signposted off the B6273 road from Nostell to Hemsworth between Kinsley and Hemsworth. The approach is unpromising: through an industrial estate. Follow the brown signs to a large car-park. To the right is a large lake with lots of ducks and geese. Beyond the far end of the car-park on the left is Playworld, a large adventure playground with a miniature railway with train rides, large tower slide, swings, see-saws, "toddlers' dell", playboat and cableway, open from Easter to September.

At the head of the lake is the Windsurfer pub, where there are toilets. Pedaloes can be hired here too.

Vale Head Park is a small, but attractive park, with streams, gardens, a children's playground, open all year and free, a golf course, a crazy golf course, two bowling greens and pleasant paths.

Our walk of 1¼ miles (2 kms) combines some of the attractions of both parks. Explorer 278.

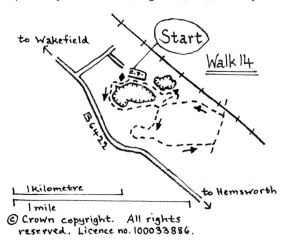

By   bus: 196/223496/498 Wakefield-Hemsworth, 244/245 Pontefract-Barnsley. *By car:* car-park at the Water Park.

From the car-park walk past the front of the Windsurfer pub on the path which leads anti-clockwise round the large lake. When the tarmac path starts, immediately fork left off it to stay by the lake. The path soon leads you up some steps, at the top of which it forks: keep left. There are lots of grassy areas and benches here. The large lake is below you on the left. When you reach a junction with a couple of benches in front of you, turn left. In a few yards the path forks: the left hand branch leads down to a "beach", but we keep right.

Cross a wooden footbridge out of the Water Park and into Vale Head Park, and immediately in front of you is the children's playground. Bear left past a bollard and turn right on a tarmac path with the fence of the play area on your right and a beck to your left. Ignore a path forking left across the beck and continue up to a shelter, with a small

43

pond on the left. Just past this keep right at the fork, straight uphill. Above the play area is the crazy golf course.

The right-hand of the two red-brick buildings ahead is a toilet block. But 20 yards before you reach it turn right off the path, over the grass, keeping the crazy golf fence on your right. Where this turns right, bear left towards a bowling green and walk anti-clockwise round it. Walk round three sides of it and you will reach a path which winds up on the right and adjacent to it a flight of steps winding up through bushes. Take either of these (the steps can be slippery!). They meet up at another bowling green. Walk anti-clockwise round this one too until you reach an exit by the railings in the far corner and emerge onto a broad tarmac drive.

The red-brick toilets are to your left. Cross the broad drive diagonally left and walk down another broad tarmac drive with gardens and the tennis court to your right. When you spot a narrow stone bridge across the beck down half right, fork right through the gardens down to it. Cross the bridge and keep right at the fork. A path comes in from the left as your path climbs and bends left and emerges from the rhododendrons. When you reach a sort of platform, turn right on a tarmac path through the grass.

The path begins to descend gently and another path comes in from the left. Keep forward towards the trees. At the trees the path bears right and the concrete surface ends. Follow the path out of the trees and along with a low embankment on the right, until you reach a cross path coming down some brick steps on the right. Turn left down the field boundary towards a railway tunnel you can see ahead. The golf course is on your left.

Don't go through the tunnel, but 20 yards before it turn left to walk along the right hand edge of the golf course, with a metal fence on your right. When the fence turns off right, keep forward on a clear path through the wood. Follow the path until 20 yards ahead of you you see the fence corner of the children's playground which you passed earlier: at this point fork right and pass between two wooden posts, with the Water Park's smaller lake visible ahead. Ignore a path forking left, but a few yards further on at the T-junction turn right.

Keep along the edge of the wood. The path curves left in the wood to reach the lake: bear left on the grass round the side of the lake. There is actually a path about five yards in from the lake. This path bears left through a little copse. Keep along on the grass by the lakeside until you reach a slightly better path coming in from the left and the large lake is over to your left. Cross a broad bridge and fork left (by forking right you would reach Playworld). Follow this path back to the start.

15. Stanley Marsh Nature Reserve and the Aire & Calder Navigation

4 miles (6½ km); Explorer 289. Green paths, wildlife, a fine old hall, a canal and marina and lots more to explore.

By bus: No. 443/446 (Leeds - Wakefield- Barnsley) to Lime Pit Lane. Walk up it to the Reserve car-park.
By car: Follow the A642 Wakefield to Oulton road. Turn left into Lime Pit Lane (signposted to Lee Moor, Lofthouse Gate and Outwood), proceed for 200 yards, pass the renovated property on the left and immediately after it park in the Reserve car-park, which is not signposted and easy to miss.

Go through the gate and follow the path into the wood. At the T-junction where the boardwalk begins turn left and climb the hill. At the observation platform see what birds you can identify on the lake. Continue through the wood. A path from the road comes in from the left and looking right there is a fork: take the left hand path. Follow the path through grassland, ignore a path forking off right, and shortly afterwards pass through a kissing-gate into trees. Immediately after the gate take the right fork; soon you are joined by a path from the left, a few yards after which ignore a cross path and keep straight on along the narrow strip of woodland with Normanton Golf Course on both sides.

At the fork keep left over the footbridge, cross straight over the tarmac road and follow the broad gravel track. Look out for flying golf balls where a fairway crosses the track. The large house on the right beyond the golf course is Hatfeild Hall. Where the track bends left and then right again turn sharp left and follow a wall on your left. When the track bends right through the hedge, keep straight ahead by the wall. The path leads through the remains of a kissing-gate and still has the wall on the left. At the T-junction (by a footpath sign and with a wooden fence straight ahead) turn right, and soon right again into a fenced path. At the end of the fence turn left and pass under the power lines. When the path forks keep right, passing under the power lines again and soon with a hedge to your right. The path becomes enclosed and tree-lined.

At the road turn left and at the next junction, with an entrance to Pinderfields Hospital ahead, turn left down Bar Lane to the A642. Turn right and cross the A642 at the pedestrian crossing. Turn right for a few yards and walk down the drive of Clarke Hall for a look at this fine old 16th-17th century house, which groups of schoolchildren now visit to experience life as it was lived in olden days Return to the main road, turn right and take the footpath on the right before the entrance to the Hospice. Follow the footpath until the pond is reached

Walk 15

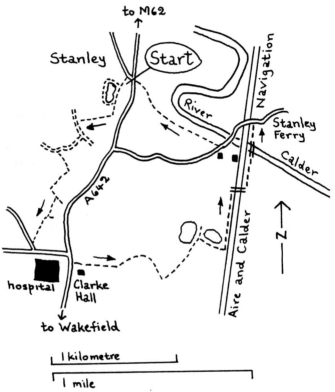

1 kilometre

1 mile

on the left and walk along its right hand side until you reach a cross track. Turn right across the plank bridge, then immediately fork half-left off the track onto the footpath by the reed-covered lake, walking towards the pylon. Look out for the herons.

Pass through a kissing-gate and turn left along the Aire and Calder Navigation. Cross it by Ramsdens Bridge (before you cross, notice the swing bridge). Ahead are two aqueducts where the canal crosses the River Calder. The iron construction was opened in 1839 and was the first suspension aqueduct to be built in the world. Cross the river by a bridge to the right of the aqueducts and walk along by the canal, then climb the steps to the road, turn left and cross the canal by the road bridge. Cross the river again by Stanley Ferry Bridge, from which there is an excellent view of the old aqueduct.

A few yards further on are the entrances to the marina and the Mill House Inn: here there are food, drinks, swings and climbing frames. Return to the road, cross it and take the footpath immediately opposite. This is the Nagger Line (from Navigation Line), formerly a railway used to bring coal from Lofthouse to the Navigation and now part of the Trans-Pennine Trail, a walking and cycling route from Liverpool to Hull. Follow it to the A642 and cross into Lime Pit Lane to return to the car-park.

(As an optional extra you could go through the gate again, turn right at the first junction and walk completely round the lake. This takes half an hour.)

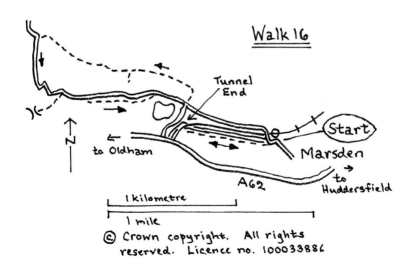

Walk 16

Tunnel End

to Oldham

N

Start

Marsden

to Huddersfield

A62

1 kilometre

1 mile

16. Tunnel End and Close Gate Bridge

The Huddersfield Narrow Canal was designed to provide a link between the Ashton Canal at Ashton-under-Lyne with the Huddersfield Broad Canal at Huddersfield and thus make possible a third crossing of the Pennines by water (the other two were the Rochdale Canal and the Leeds and Liverpool Canal). It was a troublesome and expensive undertaking which never really paid off economically. The biggest construction problem was the Standedge tunnel, the longest canal tunnel ever built in Britain, which was completed in 1810; it is 5,198 metres (3 miles, 406 yards) long.

Not long after the canal was completed, competition from the railway started, and in 1845 the canal company ceased to operate as a separate company, amalgamating with the railway company as the Huddersfield and Manchester Railway and Canal Company. Today the towpath on both sides of the tunnel (there was never a towpath through the tunnel, the boats being "legged" through), from Huddersfield to Marsden and Diggle to Ashton is a fascinating walk through part of Yorkshire and Lancashire's industrial heritage and through some characteristic and bleak Pennine countryside.

5,685 acres of this countryside, in the northern part of the Peak District National Park, is owned by the National Trust as their Marsden Moor Estate, with valleys, reservoirs, peaks and crags. It supports large numbers of moorland birds, such as the golden plover, red grouse, curlew and twite and is a designated SSSI which forms part of an international Special Area of Conservation. At the estate office in the Standedge Visitor Centre car-park at Marsden Station the Trust has a "Welcome to Marsden" exhibition, a small but informative display about the area, its natural and industrial heritage. Here too you can pick up a guided walks leaflet, a pocket guide to Marsden including 6 self-guided walks and a heritage trail covering Tunnel End and Marsden village. It is open all year round. The Standedge Visitor Centre itself, which is at Tunnel End itself, is open in summer.

By train: To Marsden Station (Huddersfield to Manchester Victoria line).
By car: Park in the Standedge Visitor Centre car-park beside Marsden Station.

Explorer OL21 South Pennines. The walk is of 3 miles (5 km). It is quite strenuous, as it climbs high up the valley side before dropping steeply back to the valley bottom. The highlight of the walk is an old packhorse bridge which makes a fine spot for picnics and paddling.

Near the entrance to the car-park and just below the station there is access to the canal towpath (heading west, i.e. with the station on your right) at Lock 42 East, the highest lock on the canal. Follow the towpath along by the summit pound, until you pass under the railway and reach a winding-hole opposite the old canal warehouse. Cross the canal by the bridge: looking left you can see the entrance to the tunnel with the former Tunnel Keepers' Cottages, soon once more to be the Standedge Visitor Centre.

Tunnel End

Follow the road up past the entrance to the old warehouse to the Tunnel End Inn. Cross straight over Waters Road and take the cobbled lane to the right of the pub, but turn left along the path behind it. Pass through a gate and continue with a wall on the left towards a cluster of houses. When the wall ends, turn sharp right up some steps and follow a wall on the right up to a track. Turn left along it.

When you reach the houses, keep right where the track forks. Soon the lane passes through another cluster of houses. When you reach a junction, take the tarmac lane forking right. In a few yards it bends sharp left again. At the next houses the tarmac ends. Pass round the back of the second house into a walled footpath. When this ends at a gateway, keep forward across open grassland. Notice the remains of paving on this old path. At a fork of sorts keep right on the higher, clearer path.

You are now high above the valley. Pass through a gate and follow the path as it winds down and up. Pass a demolished building and drop to cross a beck by a footbridge. Turn left and climb, with the remains of a wall on the right, to a large gate and a tarmac road. Turn left. After a time the road descends steeply into the valley. Just after passing Eastergate Cottage on the left turn sharp right down a signposted bridleway. The beck is below you on the left. You reach a picturesque old packhorse bridge, near which you will find pleasant spots to picnic and paddle.

This packhorse road, Rapes Highway, follows a route across the bleak moors to Rochdale. The bridge is shown on maps as Close Gate Bridge, but locally it is named after Esther Schofield, a former keeper of the nearby Packhorse Inn. "Esther's Gate" became "Eastergate". "Close Gate" means "the road to the cloughs", the narrow upland valleys.

From the bridge retrace your steps to the road. Walk down the road and keep straight on at the crossroads. Shortly after passing a terrace of houses at Lower Hey Green, a gateway on the right at a layby gives access to a well-used permissive path by the beck. Shortly, when faced by a side beck, the path bears left, crosses a stone footbridge, then bears right again down to resume its course along the beck. After a time the path climbs a low embankment to continue between the beck down on the right and a water channel to the left.

When you are faced by the stone embankment of the former Tunnel End canal Reservoir, bear left up to the road and turn right along it, in a few yards reaching once more the Tunnel End Inn. Turn right and immediately fork left to return to the canal. Cross the bridge and turn left along the towpath. Immediately after you have passed under the railway bridge, turn right up some steps. At the top bear left past benches and a picnic table to follow a woodland path along a disused railway track. Having gone through a stile by a gate, bear left to rejoin the towpath and follow it back to the start of the walk.

Close Gate Bridge

17. Digley Reservoir

3 miles (5 km); Explorer 288. The walk uses attractive paths and old tracks and includes the circuit of the reservoir; there are good views and the scenery is beautiful.

By bus: No.310 from Huddersfield to Holme (daily, hourly).
By car: From the A6024 in Holmbridge, almost opposite the parish church, take Field End Lane beside the Bridge Inn. At the first fork keep left on Bank Top Lane. Soon the high reservoir dam appears ahead: don't cross it, but keep straight on and in a short distance turn left into Digley Quarry car-park. Leave the car-park up a ramp to a gap in a wall, turn right up the track and start the walk at [*].

From the cobbled square in the centre of Holme walk up the lane away from the main road (Meal Hill Road), passing a children's playground, and where the lane bends slightly left, opposite a house on the left called The Nook, go through an iron gate on the right

The playground in Holme

into a walled track. You can easily touch the roof of the building on the right. At the end of the track squeeze through the narrow stile by the gate and cross the field diagonally to a stile in the far corner (fine views down the Holme valley and over to the Emley Moor mast), then follow the wall on the right along to another narrow old snicket. (Some parents may need to go on a diet before tackling this walk!)

A clear path leads across the next two fields, dropping right in the second to a stile in the bottom corner. Now follow the wall on the right along, crossing a muddy beck on the way, to the next stile, bear half-right to a snicket lower down in the next wall, then cross the next field to a wooden stile. Now the path keeps forward for a short distance, then bears right quite steeply down the field to join a clear cross path.

Turn right, with the reservoir down on your left, and follow this clear path to a car park and the road. Turn left and cross the dam, and on the far side turn left with the road. When the road bends right, go through a kissing-gate on the left (signposted Picnic Site avoiding road) onto a path which soon climbs steps to another kissing-gate and a track, with the picnic site beyond. Here motorists will find their

Walk 17

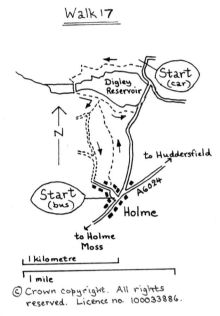

cars. Notice the fine row of "weaver's windows" in the house at the top of the hill above the quarry. Turn left up the walled track.

[*] At the top of the slope the lane opens out briefly: bear left with it downhill again, ignoring a gap in the wall on the right into another quarry. A few yards before it ends, fork right off it on a clear path, soon with a wood on the left. Descend a flight of steps to reservoir level, after which the path soon resumes as a walled track. Where the track divides, by a bench, go down left, soon turning sharp left through a metal gate and dropping to cross the dam between Digley and Bilberry Reservoirs. Follow the narrow path steeply up the other side to a gate at the top, from where the path leads along with the reservoir far below. Go through a gate by a bench and follow the path to another gate just before a footbridge.

Do not go through the gate. Immediately before it turn right up an old walled lane with the beck on the left. Cross a stile and follow the lovely (but sometimes wet and muddy – and slippery!) path as it winds up through bracken and bilberries and heather. When you emerge from the trees you have an old wall and fence to your right. You reach a track on a bend: bear left along it. There now follows a long, but gentle climb with fine views. Shortly after passing through a stile by a gate you reach a junction: bear left down this wider track, passing Meal Hill (a house!) and the village school to the centre of Holme village and the bus. Motorists should now jump to the start of the walk description for the route back to their car.

Digley Reservoir

"follow the narrow path steeply up the other side..."

18. Castle Hill

This magnificent viewpoint, which now overlooks Huddersfield, was adopted by Iron Age people for a hill-fort, and some of the conspicuous banks and ditches may have originated at that time. They are worth exploring. Later this was the site of a Norman motte-and-bailey castle, built by the de Lacy family around 1140. The Jubilee Tower itself was built for Queen Victoria's 60th Jubilee in 1897, and rebuilt and repaired in 1960 and for Queen Elizabeth II's Silver Jubilee in 1977. The top of the tower is just over 1000 feet above sea level.

2¼ miles (3¾ km); Explorer 288. The walk is quite strenuous, with a long climb up and a descent which includes a long flight of steps.

Castle Hill

St. John's Church stands beside the traffic lights at the crossroads in Newsome, 1 mile south of the centre of Huddersfield. If travelling from Huddersfield by car along Newsome Road, go straight on at the lights and park on the roadside between the church and the church hall, which is on the left of Newsome Road South 100 yards ahead. There is also a bus stop by the hall, for route 306 from Huddersfield (frequent). It saves a little pavement walking to get off the bus two stops further down Newsome Road South, opposite Plantation Drive. There is a bus shelter nearby for services back to Huddersfield at the end of the walk.

From the church hall walk downhill on the left hand side of Newsome Road South. The houses end and there is a good view up to our goal, the tower on Castle Hill. Opposite Plantation Drive turn left down the steps and follow the wall on the left. Cross the beck by the footbridge and climb straight up the field to the next road.

Turn left on the road, then in 100 yards turn sharp right into Cold Hill Lane, which curls round the hillside giving splendid views. Clockwise from the tall mast of Holme Moss, which is ahead and slightly to the right, you will see the conical hump of West Nab rising above the ridge of Deer Hill, the sharp rightwards drop of Deer Hill End above Marsden, two tall masts on Pole Moor, some smaller masts on Scapegoat Hill, the new schools at Newsome on the grassy hill nearby just across Newsome Road South (from some points on the lane you can see traffic on the M62 motorway in the dip of the skyline above the schools) and the long white block of the Royal Infirmary at Lindley.

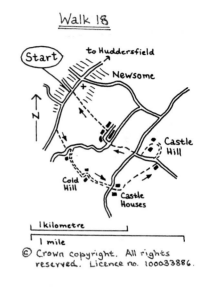

Walk 18

Follow the lane which passes between buildings at Cold Hill - the tower on Castle Hill is nicely framed between them. When the tarmac surface ends, continue up the track, quite a stiff climb, to the next road, Ashes Lane. Turn right for 50 yards, then turn left on a lane called Castle Houses. Pass Castle House Farm. Walk through the farmyard and in the far left corner enter a walled green lane. When the lane turns right 40 yards further on, cross a stile on the left and follow the wall on your right along. Make for a white house, crossing several stiles on the way. Pass immediately to the left of the house to reach Lumb Lane.

Turn left, and in 50 yards pass a tarmac drive on the right, then a few yards further on turn right onto the tarmac road (Hill Side) which soon curves left up to the summit of Castle Hill. Walk past the new hotel building and the Armada Beacon and up to the base of the Jubilee Tower.

Walk past the Tower to descend by a long flight of steps and turn right along the road at the bottom. At the T-junction cross straight over to the stile opposite and walk down the first field close to the right hand edge. In the second field cross diagonally left to join a track in the bottom corner; this leads down to the next road.

Cross straight over into Hall Bower. Follow this round a right hand bend, keep left at the fork and in about 75 yards, opposite a telegraph pole standing just over the field wall on your right, turn left between the cottages, onto a very pleasant surfaced path, which leads all the way back to Newsome Road South beside the church hall.

19. The Kirklees Light Railway

The Kirklees Light Railway is a 15-inch gauge line about 4 miles long using steam locomotives. The round trip from the terminus at Clayton West takes about 50 minutes. It is open every weekend throughout the year, every day from the end of May to the beginning of September and on most school holidays (the telephone number for enquiries is 01484-865727). Trains run each hour starting at 11 a.m. At the terminus there are a large free car-park, a café, a children's play area, fairground rides, a passenger-carrying model railway around the duckpond and a souvenir shop strong on Thomas the Tank Engine products.

I suggest that you take the train from Clayton West to the terminus at Shelley and walk back. This would be an easy and attractive, mainly rural walk of 3¾ miles (6 km). If that is too far, then stay on the train and get off at one of the intermediate halts (be sure you tell the driver where you want to get off, or he may not stop!) and walk back from there (but the nicest bit of the walk is the bit from Shelley!). From Skelmanthorpe the walk would be just over 2 miles (3¼ km) and from Cuckoo's Nest just over 1 mile (1¾ km). Explorer 288.

By bus: 235 Huddersfield-Barnsley, 240 Huddersfield-Clayton West, 935 Wakefield-Holmfirth, 447/448 Leeds-Wakefield-Denby Dale.
By car: The "narrow gauge scenic railway" is signposted off the A636 Wakefield to Denby Dale road at Clayton West.

I wonder if Shelley Station is the only one in the country with no legal exit on foot! Everyone is expected to travel back by train. So our walk starts with a little bit of innocent trespass! Walk past the turntable at

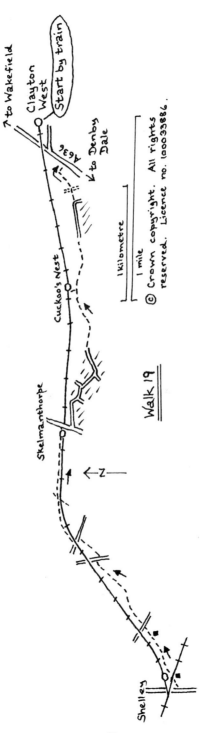

Start by train

↗ to Wakefield

Clayton West

A636

← to Denby Dale

Cuckoo's Nest

Skelmanthorpe

← N →

Shelley

Walk 19

1 Kilometre

1 mile

© Crown copyright. All rights
reserved. Licence no. 100035686.

the end of the line and take the right hand of the two tracks which face you. This descends to a large gate, which is likely to be locked: slim youngsters may be able to squeeze past it, Mums and Dads will have to climb it! Turn left at the road and immediately pass under two railway bridges. The second of these carries the Denby Dale/Penistone line from Huddersfield to Sheffield.

80 yards beyond the second bridge cross a stone step-stile on the left and walk up the left hand edge of the field to another stile at the top. Cross this and walk straight forward to the railway bridge ahead. Here you cross *over* the Denby Dale line. The track passes through a gate – there is a stile to the left of the tree – and when the fence on the left turns sharp left, bear half left to a stile, passing a large gate which, as you will notice, almost but not quite gives access to Shelley Station!

Cross the stile and follow the left hand edge of several fields, crossing several stiles, to pass to the left of a large shed, through a farmyard – the large dog is securely fastened and can't quite reach you! – and down the farm access road. Cross straight over the road at the bottom to the track opposite and follow this old walled lane all the way to the next road. On the way, where another track comes through a gate on the left, you might like to go through a gap in the wall on the left to see far below the start of the tunnel you came through earlier on the train.

At the next road turn right for 40 yards, then go through the gap-stile on the left into an enclosed path, which soon passes a large, attractive pond. A school and its playing fields are over the hedge on the right. At the next road cross straight over into an unofficial, but well-used path. Shortly you will see the railway, which has just emerged from the tunnel, far below on the right. The tunnel entrance (or exit) can be clearly seen. The path runs parallel to the railway.

At one point ignore a stile in the wall on the left and a walled footpath descending on the right. When you reach a cross track, with a railway bridge on the right, cross diagonally left to a stile opposite. Follow the path along, and when you reach a fork by a bench, keep right. Pass a redundant kissing-gate and follow the path to Skelmanthorpe Station. Just before the high bridge bear left up to the road.

If you get off the train at Skelmanthorpe Station, walk towards the high stone bridge, turn left through a gap in the fence and follow the track up to the road. Turn sharp right, cross the road and walk up the footway, passing over the railway. Take the first street on the left, Savile Road (misspelt!). The road bends right at Dawson's Mill; follow it to the top of the next hill and turn left along Pilling Lane past Skelmanthorpe Methodist Church.

The tarmac surface soon ends. Ignore a footpath forking left near the end of the houses and soon you are heading out into the country once more on a walled track. After a time a track comes in from the left from Cuckoo's Nest. (If you are only walking back from Cuckoo's Nest, when you get off the train, take the path down through the wood, walk down some steps at the bottom onto a track, cross this diagonally right to a stile and turn left up another track, passing under the railway, to a cross track at the top. Turn left.)

Follow the track to the next houses and keep forward down the road. Where the road turns right, pass round the barrier straight ahead and follow a high fence on the right to a field with a football pitch (beyond the football pitch there are swings and a slide). Keep along the left hand edge of the field, cross a farm track by stiles and follow the clear path across the middle of the next field. When you reach a fence corner by some trees, ignore a path forking left across the field. Keep forward, and soon you cross the beck on the right by a footbridge. Follow the path up to the main road and turn left. Cross where convenient and turn right up Park Mill Way, which leads back to the start.

Walk 20

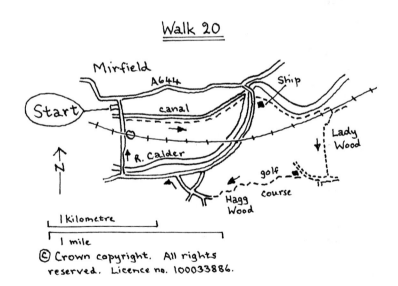

59

20. The Calder & Hebble Navigation, Lady Wood and Hagg Wood

A canal through the Calder valley was first mooted in 1740, but at first it was opposed by the mill owners, who thought it would deprive them of the water they needed for their mills. They came round to the idea however and in 1758 an Act of Parliament was passed to make the River Calder navigable from Wakefield to Salterhebble (in 1768 the canal was extended to Sowerby Bridge, where it connected with the trans-Pennine Rochdale Canal). The builder was John Smeaton, who also built the Eddystone lighthouse, helped by the canal expert James Brindley.

The walk starts in Mirfield, follows the canal towpath to the Marina at Shepley Bridge Lock, passes the Ship Inn, where there is a large children's play area, then follows old tracks through the woods south of the Calder, which can be muddy. It is 3¼ miles (5¼ km) long. Explorer 288.

By bus: There are buses from Huddersfield, Leeds, Dewsbury, Bradford and Wakefield to Mirfield. Get off at the Library and walk down Station Road. Cross the canal and turn left along the towpath.

By train: There are trains from Huddersfield, Dewsbury, Leeds and Wakefield to Mirfield on the Huddersfield line. Leave the station and walk up Station Road towards the centre of Mirfield, and at the canal turn right down to the towpath.

By car: Park in the car park behind Mirfield Library (pay-and-display), walk down Station Road, cross the canal and turn left along the towpath.

Follow the towpath of the Calder & Hebble Navigation to the lock and marina at Shepley Bridge. There are always many boats to be inspected here. Cross the bridge over the canal to the road, then turn right over the bridge over the river Calder. Turn left into the car park of the Ship Inn (there is a large play area behind the pub), walk straight across it and continue along a paved track. Deep wheel ruts in the paving stones testify to much use in earlier times. Follow the path along the river bank. At a fork keep right on the clearer, ascending path, then turn left alongside the railway. Cross the railway bridge and keep straight ahead through the barrier into Lady Wood.

Follow the track up through the wood; soon old paving begins. On leaving the wood, continue up the fenced, paved track. There are usually lots of horses in the fields around here, which is why the woodland tracks can be very muddy. The track bends right. Pass between two old stone gateposts and keep forward, towards a large complex of stone buildings. There's a good view over the Calder valley. When you reach a tarmac road, keep forward along it, and immediately before the buildings fork left, cross the stile by the gate and walk up the right hand edge of the field.

Cross the stile in the top corner – be careful not to touch the fences, which may be electrified – and walk down the narrow walled footpath. Walk straight over two fairways of the Dewsbury & District Golf Club's course – play is from right to left on the first one, from left to right on the second – into the wood, and turn right down the cross track, ignoring tracks to left and right back onto the golf course. This is where the mud may begin! At the time of writing the bottom of the track is obstructed by a fallen tree, but normally one would walk down until faced by a blocked gate, at which point you would turn left between stone gateposts to follow the path through Hagg Wood. Follow the path as directly as possible through the wood to the far side.

At one point it is at present blocked by another fallen tree, but this can easily be by-passed. Here the path forks: keep right, descending gently, in a few yards being joined by another path from the right: turn left along this broad path. At the next junction bear right into a hollow way, which leads down to the exit from the wood. Pass between two large stone gateposts and continue down the walled lane. At the next junction keep straight forward along the road, and when you reach another one, with the entrance to New Hall Farm on the left and a red post box to the right, keep straight forward along the road.

When you reach the main road (Granny Lane), turn left along the footway, and at the next main junction fork right to cross the Calder once more, then follow the road back to the centre of Mirfield.

Baitings Reservoir

21. Two Reservoir Walks

Explorer OL21, South Pennines. The shorter walk (just under 1½ miles, 2¼ km) is a circuit of Baitings Reservoir; it is level, through woodland, an interesting path to follow, and there are several benches at what would be attractive picnic spots. The longer walk (3 miles, 4¾ km) makes a circuit of the adjacent Ryburn Reservoir, but it does not follow the bank; it is more strenuous, with more ups and downs, including flights of steps, but is more varied and has much better views; parts of it can be muddy after wet weather. Both walks make use of Yorkshire Water Permissive Paths.

Both walks start from an unsignposted Yorkshire Water car-park by the dam of Baitings Reservoir on the A58 Halifax-Rochdale road. The entrance is by a disused toilet block, almost opposite a house with a large sundial over the door, which is dated 1764 (Baitings Cottage). The 528 Halifax-Rochdale bus stops opposite this house.

The shorter walk. Climb the steps from the car-park to the A58 and turn left. 40 yards past the bus stop go through a stile on the left, signposted Permissive Path to Causeway and Manshead Hill, go down three steps and take the path parallel to the bank of the reservoir. Having walked the length of the reservoir you climb a few steps and emerge through a gateway onto a road. Turn left to cross the causeway.

On the far side go through another gateway on the left onto the path which leads back along the other side of the reservoir. Eventually you will reach a gate at the end of the dam. Cross the dam to return to your starting point.

The longer walk. From the corner of the car-park below the old toilet block go through the kissing-gate and walk down the fenced path. At the foot of the slope it turns left, parallel to a tarmac road, which soon bends away right. When the fenced path approaches the end of a building, it bends right and continues to descend. Ryburn Reservoir is seen in the distance. The path passes between two pairs of large wooden gates, after the second of which it drops steeply by steps towards the River Ryburn.

At the bottom turn left over a ladder stile and follow the path with the "river" to your right. Cross a step stile and another ladder stile close together, and ignoring the footbridge to your right, turn left to continue along the permissive path. After passing some heather covered crags, the path reaches the reservoir and follows its bank. Cross a side valley by a footbridge, accompanied by a large pipe. Eventually a stile by a gate leads into a field. Walk straight over the field to the stile by the gate opposite.

Turn right down the steps. There are picnic tables on the right, and at the far end of the car-park on the left there are toilets, which may be open, but don't count on it! Cross the reservoir dam. At the far side bear right along the path, which passes more picnic tables, and becomes broad track. At the end of this arm of the reservoir cross the footbridge on the right and follow the path up through the wood. Cross the stile at the top and continue uphill with a wall on your right.

Walk 21

Go through the gated stile in the top corner and continue up the walled path. At the farm go through a gate, pass to the right of the buildings, go through another gate and keep on up the fenced path to a stile. Go diagonally right for a couple of yards to the next stile, then continue uphill with the wall/fence on your right. In the top corner of this field cross the stile and keep on in the same direction as before in an enclosed path. Go through a gap stile ahead (there is a step stile in the fence on the left here) and continue up the enclosed path.

Where the old walled lane turns sharp left go through the gate in the wall on the right and walk down the slope to the ruined farm, there turning left to walk through between the buildings. Ignore footpath signs pointing right and left, and keep forward, soon with a wall to your right. Baitings dam is half-right ahead. Soon you are in a double walled lane, which leads round to the right of the next farm (Higher Wormald). Now you have a choice of route. The shorter one goes through the kissing-gate to the right of the access track and aims downhill to the next farm, there crossing the yard and turning right down the grassy track. For better views (but with more ascent!) walk up the access track to the next road, there turning right downhill and taking the first walled lane on the right, which leads you past the same farm and into the grassy track, which leads to the dam. Cross this to return to your starting point.

Baitings Reservoir

Hebble Hole Bridge (Walk 22)

22. Heptonstall and the Colden Valley

An exploration of a well-preserved hilltop Pennine village, now a Conservation Area, and a walk into a beautiful side valley of the Calder with many remains of the early Industrial Revolution. Stroll round the village 1 mile (1.5 km), walk proper 3 miles (5 km). Explorer OL21.

By bus: 591 Halifax-Hebden Bridge-Heptonstall (Mon-Sat hourly). On reaching the village centre, the bus turns left: stay on it until you approach a children's playground. Walk on in the same direction to reach the visitors' car-park at the end of the road.

By car: As you approach from Hebden Bridge and the Calder valley, at the entrance to the village a visitors' car-park is signposted to the left. Follow the road, passing a children's playground on the left, which you may like to visit later, to the large car-park of the Heptonstall Social and Bowling Club at the end.

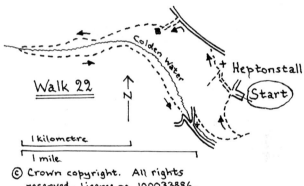

© Crown copyright. All rights reserved. Licence no. 100033886.

To explore Heptonstall village, leave the Visitors' Car-park and take the walled lane opposite. A few yards before you reach the first cross street, follow the footpath sign pointing left along a track. Cross a cobbled street and follow the path to the rim of the Colden Valley. This is a superb viewpoint. To the left in the distance can be seen Stoodley Pike Monument, first constructed shortly after the Battle of Waterloo. In the Calder valley the Rochdale Canal, the railway and the former turnpike road share the narrow space available. On the left hand hillside above the railway viaduct is a rocky outcrop, to the left of which there was in the Middle Ages an extensive hunting park.

Retrace your steps and keep forward to the church. Bear left, enter the churchyard by the gate on the right and bear left round the tower, passing a large stone pinnacle, which fell when the church was struck by lightning in 1875. Turn left, to leave the churchyard again, and turn right along Church Street.

An old packhorse road in the Colden Valley

The large house on the right is the Vicarage, on the site of which was once the cock-pit (see plaque). At the next cross street the main walk turns left up the hill out of the village. Straight ahead are toilets, open in summer. Turn right down the cobbled main street past the White Lion. The Cloth Hall on the right is where pieces of woollen cloth produced by local hand-loom weavers were taken for sale to dealers. Turn left along Northgate. Notice the carved stone on New House, dated 1736, with the initials of the builders, Henry and Elizabeth Foster (see page 6). A little further along on the right is access to the octagonal Methodist church, built in 1764.

Weavers' Square, Heptonstall

Continue along Northgate to a signposted footpath on the right down a few steps. It passes to the left of the Methodist church. There is a fine view of the Hebden Valley ahead.

At the next junction turn right. Just before you reach the car-park, the walled enclosure on the left, now a picnic site, was the pinfold, where stray animals were impounded until their owner paid a fine for their return. Walk through the car-park. Just past a detached garage on the right, a small door indicates the former dungeon or lock-up, and a little further on you pass the Great Well, which once supplied most of the village with water.

Turn right at the main street, up past the post office. Turn left just before the Cloth Hall, signposted Museum. The Museum is in the former Grammar School, founded in 1642. Enter the churchyard and turn right up to the door of the old church. The mediaeval church was ruined in a great storm in 1847, and the new one nearby was completed in 1854.

The most famous grave is that of "King" David Hartley, who was the leader of a gang of men who forged gold coins. He was hanged in 1770. With your back to the door of the church, count forward twelve stone slabs, then two down to the left, to find his grave. The ultra-modern interior of the new church is worth a visit.

Now, for the main walk, return to the main street of the village and turn left uphill. Walk up to the top of the village and continue up the road. Just over the brow of the hill there are a couple of benches on a knoll on the left, with a fine view of the Colden Valley. Take the narrow tarmac lane just before these benches (Lumb Bank). On the way down notice where the Calderdale Way forks right off the lane. When the tarmac lane swings sharp left, keep forward down the track. You have the tall chimney of a former textile mill down to the left. When the track reaches a T-junction, turn right (signposted Public Bridleway Colden Clough).

The Colden valley

Follow the gently rising footpath and soon another tall chimney appears. Just before it the track forks: keep left downhill past the chimney. Climb a couple of steps onto the embankment of the former mill reservoir and bear left along the top of it. TAKE CARE: STEEP DROP. When you reach the end of the embankment, steps on the right lead round the overgrown remains of Bob Mill. At the top of the steps turn sharp right on the ascending packhorse path, and in a few yards sharp left again. When the path broadens out, ignore the track forking back right: keep forward along the narrower footpath through attractive open woodland.

Near the far end of the wood, where the path forks, keep right, up to the top corner. At the top ignore a step-stile back on the right: keep forward slightly downhill with a wall on your right. This is another old paved packhorse path (see page 66). Some way along ignore a steep flight of steps on the right: take rather the steps on the left, here joining the Pennine Way. CARE: STEEP DROP. Cross Hebble Hole Bridge (see page 64), built of huge slabs of stone. There is a good picnic spot on the far side, by the beck. This is also the furthest point of the walk.

From the bridge bear left with the Pennine Way (the Calderdale Way takes the right fork) up a long and steep flight of steps to a prominent signpost on the skyline. When you reach it, turn left along the track (here leaving the Pennine Way again). The walking is now easy, on a well-made, gently descending track, although it does get stonier lower down. The tower of Heptonstall Church looks a long way off from here! Pass once again the two tall chimneys.

Some way down, another track comes in from the left. Notice the remains of causeying as you descend. Follow the track all the way down to the houses of Hebden Royd. Join a tarmac road and walk down the narrow footway towards the church. Immediately before the church turn sharp left along Eaves Road past the school. Cross the bridge over Colden Water and immediately turn right along a footpath which passes the back of the school and the east end of the church. CARE! STEEP DROP! When you reach a junction – a path comes in from the left down the hill – bear right for two yards,

Another view of Hebble Hole Bridge

then with the main road straight ahead, fork left on a path which climbs through the woods.

This is the start of the climb back to Heptonstall. Take it slowly, and you'll find it's not too bad. When you reach a cross path, turn left up it. Soon you emerge from the wood and have a fine view up the Calder Valley. Pass a short, but high, stretch of wall on the right and keep on gently upwards. Notice again the remains of old paving. Pass under power lines, and a massive crag appears ahead. A few yards after the power lines turn sharply back right on a path which climbs steeply and passes back under the power lines. Pass an old stone gatepost and in two yards keep left at the fork up through grass. The path soon turns left, passes under the power lines yet again, and into a walled footpath. Turn left at the top – there's an old gate on the right – towards a telecommunications mast. Pass to the left of the mast and the visitors' car-park is on the right.

23. Shibden Valley

Shibden Hall, which lies to the north east of Halifax off the A58 road to Leeds, started life as a timber-framed house built in the early 15th century. It was partly cased in stone in the 17th century, and there were later modifications and extensions, particularly during the 19th century. The hall is now in the guardianship of the Calderdale Museums Service, who have preserved the "lived in" atmosphere, with the rooms furnished in the styles of various periods. The outbuildings and barn house the Folk Museum of West Yorkshire, where old shops, craftsmen's workshops and even a pub have been recreated. Craft demonstrations take place during the summer. The café is open all year round.

Shibden Park, the grounds of the Hall, has a large boating lake with ducks and geese, a miniature railway offering rides, a children's playground, a pitch and putt course, toilets and a refreshment kiosk.

Our walk of 3½ miles (5.6 km), one of the loveliest in the book, explores the valley of the Shibden Brook, north of the Hall and Park. The relevant map is the Explorer 288. This is easy walking, mainly on causeyed paths, tracks and minor roads, with fine views and many lovely old houses.

By bus: _No. 223, 224, 226, 508 (Leeds to Halifax); 534 (Northowram to Halifax); 509, 681, 682 (Bradford to Halifax). Alight at Stump Cross_

Inn, cross the busy road if coming from the Leeds/Bradford direction, and walk up the footway in the direction of Halifax.

By car: _Use the lower car park in Shibden Park, accessible from Godley Hill (the A58) by the gate off the lane just above the pedestrian crossing. Walk to the far end of the car park from the lake, pass round the barrier, cross the bridge and continue along the road between the houses. At the T-junction go left for a couple of yards, cross the road and climb a few steps, then bear left up the path with a high wall to the right._ **_Caution: at the top of this path is the busy main road, with no footway, so do not let young_**

"Piggate"

_children gallop ahead here__. When you reach the road, there is a layby just to the right, which will give you time to draw breath and wait_

70

for a break in the traffic before crossing the road and turning left for 10 yards.

About 20 yards before the start of the 40 m.p.h. limit take the cobbled footpath on the right, known locally as Piggate, signposted to Shibden Fold. Join a track on a bend at Shibden Fold and walk straight through between the buildings. When the track ends at Longfield Farm, keep forward through the stile and follow the paved path through three fields. The little 18th-century Spa House, which had a well which was visited by hundreds of people on May Day Pilgrimages from about 1780 to 1840, can be seen up on the left. Leave the third field by a stile (notice the iron-stained water) and keep on along the paved path, which at first runs parallel to a track and after a time joins it. Follow this all the way to the Shibden Mill Inn, built on the site of a medieval corn mill.

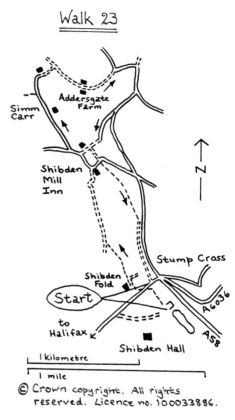

Walk through the inn car park and bear left out of it along the tarmac lane. Ignore the first lane forking right, Whiskers Lane, but at the next fork a short distance further on keep right along Simm Carr Lane, a no through road. Having passed Simm Carr Farm the wooded Simm Carr Clough is below on the left, while beyond it is the imposing Scout Hall, built in 1680. Notice a flight of steps on the left, leading down to an old stone footbridge, used by the Calderdale Way, but keep on along the lane. When the tarmac ends at Lower Lime House, keep forward up the stony track, ignoring a track forking left just past the house. At the next fork go right, and now you can begin to enjoy the views.

Follow the track straight through Addersgate Farm and along Addersgate Lane. When you reach the next tarmac road, keep forward along it (Paddock Road), bending sharp right by a water trough. A short distance further on notice the gigantic stone wall on the left. This is a fine example of the walls which were built at many local quarries to retain the excavated over-burden. At the next fork keep right down Brow Lane, and opposite No.60 take the tarmac lane forking right (Whiskers Lane). The large beams in the wall of the first house on the right reveal that it is timber-framed. When the tarmac ends keep on down the footpath. Near the foot, where the tarmac begins again, take the walled lane on the left (The Dicken), noticing

The Shibden valley

the large rutted flagstones.

Cross straight over the next road, through the stile by the gate, and follow the track forward through the fields, passing through another stile on the way. Near the far end again notice how carriage wheels have rutted the causey stones. Another stile leads out onto a tarmac lane. Walk forward along it, and when you reach the next junction keep on by the wall on your right into a descending cobbled lane. When the lane levels out you pass the 17th-century Staups House on the left. Soon you are back at the A58 and the bus stops. To return to

the car park, cross the road with great care and turn right to the far end of the layby, where you will find on the left the path that you used at the start of the walk.

Staups House

24. Ogden Water

Explorer OL21 South Pennines. Ogden Water is located 4 miles north of Halifax off the A629 Keighley road. The 502 bus runs hourly from Huddersfield/Halifax and Keighley; alight at the Causeway Foot Inn and walk along Ogden Lane to the reservoir. By car drive along Ogden Lane and at the end there are car-parks on the right, at various levels.

Near the reservoir there is a Visitor Centre, where refreshments are available, an Activity Pack and Wildlife Colouring Cards can be bought and a free leaflet with a map of the paths in the vicinity of the reservoir can be picked up. Opposite are toilets. Designated a Local

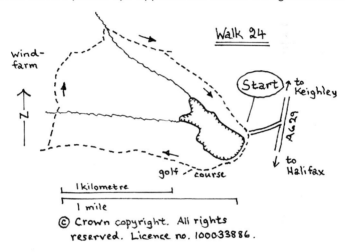

Walk 24

Wind-farm

Start — to Keighley

N

golf course

to Halifax

1 kilometre

1 mile

Nature Reserve in 2003, the Ogden Estate comprises a 34 acre reservoir, constructed in the mid-19th century, which supplies drinking water to Halifax, enclosed by 174 acres of woodland with open moor beyond.

The 1¼ mile (2 km) path round the perimeter of the reservoir is suitable for pushchairs. Our walk of 3 miles (5 km), is not, as it crosses heather moorland, at its best in August when the heather is in bloom, and where you are likely to hear the "Go back! Go back! Go back!" of the grouse, but liable to be wet, and includes the steep stepped descent into and ascent out of Ogden Clough, a deep ravine. The views are magnificent.

From the Visitor Centre cross the reservoir dam. On he far side go through the gate and walk up the concrete footpath. When this ends, keep on up the track between a wood on the right and Halifax Golf Course to the left. Further up there are fine views over the golf course to Halifax and the Emley Moor TV mast in the distance. As the gradient eases, you will see to your right the Ovenden Moor Windfarm, a prominent feature of the landscape for miles around. The windfarm was built in 1992; it supplies electricity to 7,000 homes.

Well before you reach the telecommunication masts and the first house, cross the stile by a gate on the right and follow the grassy track across the moor. The windfarm is to your left. The track ends at a little dam, which you cross, after which a footpath continues over the moor. You will have fun trying to work out as dry a route as possible! The views become increasingly extensive as you walk.

Eventually you cross a stile or go through a nearby kissing-gate and find yourself on the edge of Ogden Clough, a deep ravine. Make your way carefully down the steep path – there are steps to help you – and cross the dam at the foot. Usually from here a permissive path leads down to the reservoir and along its bank, but at the time of writing this has been closed due to a landslip. If it has been re-opened, do follow it down. Otherwise climb the steep flight of steps out of the ravine, and when you reach a cross path, turn right along it, in a few yards with a wall to your left.

Soon the reservoir appears again half right below you. Go through a metal gate and move on to the path to the right of the hollow way. In a few yards keep right at the fork. After a time the path bends right, down towards a wood, and becomes a track. Follow it all the way back to the start of the walk.

Ogden Water

25. The Great Wall of Todmorden

Todmorden, or "Tod" as it is familiarly called, is at the western end of Calderdale, and is a fascinating small town. It has several fine 19th century buildings, in particular the Town Hall, the Unitarian church, and Dobroyd Castle. All of these are connected to the Fielden family who were local cotton manufacturers and by the standards of the time very benevolent employers. Todmorden also has some quite unusual place names in its vicinity, such as Lumbutts, Mankinholes, and Shade. It also boasts its own Salford, and Portsmouth is nearby.

The Rochdale Canal is one of three canals that go across the Pennines, and it was the first to be completed. The whole length from Sowerby Bridge to Manchester was opened for traffic in 1804. Canals brought a valuable means of transport to places like Todmorden that could not previously be reached by boat, and in its heyday the Rochdale Canal carried nearly a million tons of goods a year, and passengers too. However, the canals were soon supplanted by the railways. Today, the canal is only used by pleasure boats, but it is an attractive sight as it twists and turns through town and country, and its towpath is a delight to walk on. The canal is also a haven for wildlife.

This short walk of 1½ miles (2½ km) or just over 2 with the option, is full of interest, for children and adults alike. Some of it is along the attractive towpath of the Rochdale Canal which sneaks its way through the town, and part of the route is close to the railway line. Explorer OL21.

By rail: Todmorden has a frequent rail service from Leeds, Bradford and Halifax, and the walk starts from the station which is very centrally situated. Grandparents might usefully note that for tickets Todmorden, despite its distance, is still in the metro zone.
By car: a few spaces might be found on the road leading up to the station, and there are small town centre car parks. Otherwise park out of the town centre on or close to the road to Burnley (A646).

Turn left after leaving the station, and find a few minutes to read the informative "Welcome to Todmorden" noticeboard on the right just before you reach the White Hart.

Turn left on the road underneath the railway arch, then immediately turn right and walk down the path that descends beside the railway viaduct. Just before the bottom you pass a sculpture with a white and red rose, the white for Yorkshire and the red for Lancashire (the boundary between the two rival counties used to go right through the middle of the town!).

Turn right along the main road, and appreciate the fine proportions of the railway viaduct as you walk underneath it. Soon you will pass the Town Hall on the left, a magnificent piece of architecture, built in 1870 in the Classical style. Note the marble sculptures all round the top of the building, some representing Yorkshire and some Lancashire. Immediately after the Town Hall cross the main road which goes to Halifax (A646), and as you cross you will catch a glimpse of a tower on a hill. This is the monument on Stoodley Pike, which was built to commemorate the Napoleonic Wars.

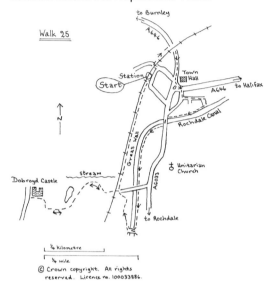

Walk 25

Now go down an attractive narrow street called Water Street (it's by a blue plaque commemorating the floods in the year 2000, and the offending small stream is at the other side of the wall). After a few yards turn left down Dale Street (by the entrance to Meadow Street there is a fine view of the Town Hall sculpture) and turn right at the end of Dale Street to reach the Rochdale Canal at "Shop Lock No 18". Again you will catch sight of Stoodley Pike.

Turn right and go along the towpath. Soon it becomes a narrow passage under Rochdale Road. Turn right immediately after and cross the bridge you have just gone under, then right again to rejoin the towpath, now on the other side of the canal. Whilst you are on the bridge, note the fine spire of the Unitarian church straight ahead. Continue along the towpath, and soon at the other side of the canal you will see an immense brick wall continuing for a considerable distance, the "Great Wall of Tod". It is an impressive structure, and it is said to have over 5 million bricks (get the children to check!).

Continue along the canal under a bridge and along another pleasant stretch of water to the next lock. You are now in Shade. Cross the footbridge over the canal, and double back on a winding tarmac path through woodland. The path eventually climbs up to the railway line.

The next part of the walk up to Dobroyd Castle is optional - and steep! (If you decide to omit it, jump straight to the next paragraph.) Cross the railway line on the level crossing (n.b. it's a busy line) and take the path that goes off to the right (beware a low metal spike!). The path has been made available for public use by the Losang

76

Dragpa Centre which owns the castle and its grounds. The path climbs steeply up the well-wooded hillside, at first beside a fast-flowing stream with a waterfall. Just after the end of the steep part, and still in the wood, a path on the right leads to an attractive large pond. After visiting the pond, continue up the path which goes by the left side of the castle and round to the front. You may see Buddhist monks, and there is also a café (not always open), and another pond. Now retrace steps to the railway crossing.

Turn left (but right, if you have balked the option!) along the fence beside the railway. Not far away on the right is a wall, and this is the top of the Great Wall, built to stop everything sliding into the canal. Very soon you are back at the station – itself a pleasant piece of architecture. If the children and you still have the energy to visit the park, keep straight on and down the path by the viaduct, then turn left along the Burnley road at the bottom, and it's about a quarter of a mile.

The Great Wall of Tod

26. Knaresborough: River, Castle and Cave

4 miles (6½ km); Explorer 289. A ramble full of interest, suitable also for folding pushchairs. The walk starts from the car park adjacent to Conyngham Hall and opposite the main entrance to the Dropping Well Estate at the bottom of the hill from Harrogate, but an alternative start could be made from the Railway Station or the Market Square, which are passed en route. Henshaws Arts and Crafts Centre on the Conyngham Hall estate is well worth a visit, with its craft shops, lots of interesting sculptures, sensory gardens, café and toilets.

Take a bus or train to Knaresborough, or if coming by car, park in the car park by Conyngham Hall.

Continue through the car park and just before you reach the picnic area turn right up the slope to the drive and turn left, soon forking right through the gateway to Conyngham Hall. Follow the drive round the front and side of the Hall, turn right, and soon among trees on the right will be seen a small cemetery for pets of the past occupants of the Hall. At the end of the high wall on the left is the entrance to Henshaws Centre. Before the main road turn right on the footpath between trees. Where this joins the open parkland turn left down a flight of steps, then left again and out to the main Harrogate-Knaresborough road by the entrance to the car park. (There are public toilets here.)

Cross the road by the pedestrian crossing, turn left, then in a few yards turn right on a cobbled road (signposted Castle and Museum) soon bearing right along The Parsonage, and on passing St John's Parish Church take the right hand footpath straight ahead. Down on the right here is the cobbled Water Bag Bank where once water was brought up from the river on pack horses for use in the town.

Cross the railway by the subway steps by the station and continue up Kirkgate. At the end, with the Tourist Information Centre just round the corner on the right, turn left and visit the historic Market Square with 'Ye Oldest Chymist Shoppe in England' - a market is held every Wednesday.

Return to the TIC, walk forward to pass to the right of the police station into the grounds of Knaresborough Castle and bear slightly right to go round the grounds in an anti-clockwise direction. Passing the great Keep you soon come to the well-known view of the River Nidd, the town and railway viaduct. Across the river is the Long Walk with the Dropping Well and Mother Shipton's Cave, which can be visited from either end on payment of an entrance fee. Further along by the War Memorial you can look down on the weir that once supplied water to the flax mill that is now converted to housing. Continue along this path, and in the middle of the grass on the left is the entrance to the Sally Port, which is a tunnel giving access to the moat below and was a secret means of getting in and out of the castle in times of siege.

On leaving the castle grounds between the two high walls of a former gate turn right (public toilets here), turn right again into Cheapside, and at the end cross by the pedestrian crossing into Windsor Lane, which becomes Stockdale Walk. Turn right opposite King James

© Crown copyright. All rights reserved. Licence no. 100033886.

Road into Crag Lane. Follow this, turn left at the end, and where the roadway ceases keep forward past the bollard along the footpath. After some considerable distance this path along the top of the cliff opens out and becomes a broad, new path edged with planks. Where this forks, keep right to reach a play area with swings and slides.

Keeping the fence of the play area on your left and fenced paddocks to your right, you reach a drive to a house ('Le Herou'). Cross it, pass through a kissing-gate and walk along a woodland path. Go through the next two kissing-gates (either side of a cross path) and continue on the path, which starts to descend. After the next kissing-gate turn right, cross a stile and emerge onto Abbey Road, where you turn left.

Over the wall on the right is the River Nidd and the Lido Caravan Park next to the old mill. At the end of the wall is an information board and a gate leading down to St Robert's Cave. Robert was a hermit who lived in the cave, and when he died in 1218 he was buried in the

79

grave that is outside the cave. So many pilgrimages were made to it that a priory was built a little way away.

Return to Abbey Road, turn left and retrace your steps for a short distance, but this time keep forward along the road with the river now on your left. This is a No Through Road so traffic should be at a minimum. Just past the road barrier, high up on a wall on the right, is a plaque giving information about the priory that gave the road its name. Just past here, low down in the garden wall on the left, can be seen stones from the dismantled priory. When the cliffs are reached on the right, next to the road are shallow caves and the holes where the roofs of simple houses slotted in. Soon over a gate on the right is the 'Chapel of Our Lady of the Crag' cut into the base of the cliff in the year 1409 with the effigy of a Crusader. A short distance further on, high up on the cliff, is the 'House in the Rock' of four rooms cut into the cliff in the 18th century.

The walk continues along Abbey Road to cross the Knaresborough-Calcutt road into Waterside. (The Mother Shipton pub is over the bridge to the left, and behind it is an entrance to the Dropping Well Estate.) Waterside is also a No Through Road, but there is a car park further along. You soon pass the converted mill and the viaduct that were seen from the castle grounds and the riverside with its cafés and ice-cream shops and a place where rowing-boats can be hired. At the end cross over the Harrogate-Knaresborough road by the pedestrian crossing and return to the car park (toilets), where those using public transport will jump to the start of the walk description.

Knaresborough

27. Harrogate: Valley Gardens, Pine Woods, Birk Crag

Harrogate is a quite a new town, certainly in comparison to its near neighbour Knaresborough. It owes its growth to its development as a spa. Its waters were first discovered in the 16th Century, but Harrogate's main period of growth was in the 19th century, when it became a major European hydropathic resort. Visitors flooded in, and many fine buildings were erected, such as the Royal Bath Hospital, the Royal Baths, and the Royal Hall. Harrogate is lent further character by the Stray, 200 acres of grassed common land encircling much of the town centre.

Our suggested walk is 4 miles (6½ km) long . Explorer 297.

By bus: There is a bus every 20 minutes from Leeds (No 67). Alight at the Monument, sometimes called the Pier (but no sea), and walk down Montpellier Parade which is down the side of Betty's.
By rail: Half hourly service from Leeds. From the station go along Cambridge Street or James Street to the Monument, then down Montpellier Parade at the side of Betty's.
By car: The most important thing is to make sure you don't get a parking fine! There are parking meters on most streets in or close to the town centre. Slightly further out, and round the entrance to the Valley Gardens is a 3 hour disk zone (disks can be bought in local shops). The safest bet is to park outside the zone, near Kent Avenue, or start the walk from the car park on Harlow Moor Road (see map).

The walk starts at the entrance to the Valley Gardens, but first, if you have time, spend half an hour in the Pump Room Museum for an interesting brief history of Harrogate, and a glass of spa water (yuk! but it is supposed to do you good). Now go into the Valley Gardens and along the main path with a stream on the left. Soon you will be in Bogs Field "a wonder of the natural world where a greater number of unique mineral springs come to the surface than at any other known place on Earth" (i.e it's a world record!). There are 36 of them, of which "no two are alike". Bogs Field, which must formerly have been a scene of muddy dribbles, is now attractive flower beds, lawns and shrubberies.

Continue in the same direction, keeping an extensive grassed area on your left. Just before woodland is reached (the Pine Woods), turn right at an information board on a path signposted to Harlow Carr Gardens. The path continues through attractive woodland (many of the trees actually *are* pines), and children can chase around and do no harm to anyone or anything. Cross Harlow Moor Road and walk through further woodland to a grassed recreational area. Continue in the same direction on a firm path, and soon you reach open country on the right with wide views. The top of Great Whernside (2310 feet, 704m), one of Yorkshire's highest hills, can be seen on a clear day.

The path comes out on a tarmac road by Harlow Carr Gardens. Turn left for the entrance to the gardens if you want to include them in the walk, otherwise turn right. Go past kennels where there is a pets corner by the road with rabbits, goats, guinea fowl, hens and other creatures (the dogs can only be heard). When the road swings right, go left through a gap in the fence to a footpath sign, and turn then right to reach Birk Crag, a pleasant airy place with a precipitous drop at the far side. After the crag the path descends steeply down steps. It turns right along a grassy terrace before reaching the bottom of the valley, and continues through attractive mixed woodland for half a mile before coming out on Cornwall Road.

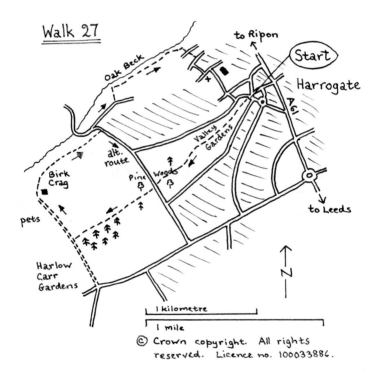

Walk 27

to Ripon

Start

Harrogate

Oak Beck

alt. route

Birk Crag

Pine Woods

pets

Valley Gardens

to Leeds

Harlow Carr Gardens

N

1 kilometre

1 mile

There are muddy sections on the next part of the walk in winter and during wet spells, so if you have an aversion to very dirty footwear, turn right along Cornwall Road, which soon leads to Harlow Moor Road, from which you can retrace your steps. Hardier walkers should turn left, then turn right at a "Ringway Footpath" sign along a wide untarmaced road. Not long after the road begins to climb, get the children to find the path that goes off to the left between houses.

The path descends through woodland to a bridge over the Oak Beck. This is the Iron Bridge, reputedly Harrogate's oldest bridge (it is thought that the bridge was used to take iron ore to nearby Kirby Overblow). It is a pity that it is now fenced off. The path, muddy and steep in places, continues down the valley through attractive woodland with frequent views of Oak Beck.

Turn right when the path comes out on to a road, and shortly afterwards at the T-junction go straight ahead up the steep footpath at the left hand side of a house. Turn right when it comes out on to Kent Road, then left along Kent Avenue with St Wilfrid's Church straight ahead. Turn left and past the church, then first right. Continue to the end of Clarence Drive, and cross the road at the T-Junction to re-enter the Valley Gardens.

Harrogate, the Valley Gardens

Brimham Rocks

28. Brimham Rocks

2¾ miles (4½ km); Explorer 298. Brimham Rocks is a wonderful natural adventure playground, owned by the National Trust, perfect for games such as hide-and-seek, for picnics and of course for clambering over rocks. There are glorious views, an Information Centre and a refreshment kiosk. This walk is an easy ramble through the moorland and farmland east of the Rocks.

No suitable public transport.
<u>*By car*</u>*: Park in the National Trust car park (fee for non-members) (GR 208 646).*

Walk back down the access drive towards the motor road, but about 40 yards before you reach it, fork right along a track signposted to Druids Cave Farm. About 10 yards before the track passes through a gateway, fork left off it along a clear path through scrubby woodland.

When you reach the road, cross straight over to the continuation of the path by a Nidderdale Way sign, and follow the clear path all the way across Brimham

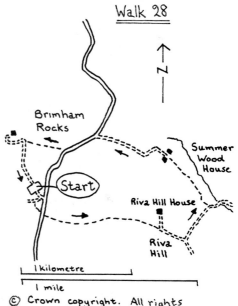

Walk 28

N

Brimham Rocks

Start

Summer Wood House

Riva Hill House

Riva Hill

| 1 kilometre |

| 1 mile |

© Crown copyright. All rights reserved. Licence no. 100033886.

Moor, at its best in August when the heather is in bloom, until you reach a stile by a gate in a wall on the far side, which marks the boundary of the National Trust land. Cross the stile and keep along with a wall to your left. Join a track coming up from Riva Hill House Farm on the left and keep forward along it. At a fork, with a wall and water trough ahead, go left through a gate into a walled lane.

Near the foot of the hill you pass through another gateway and enter woodland. About 15 yards further on fork left off the concrete track along an unsurfaced track with the beck over to your right. You have to ford a shallow side beck before the track leads you out of the wood through a gate. Keep forward along the hedge on your left. Go

85

through the gate into the yard of Summer Wood House, pass to the right of the house and follow the concrete access drive as it bears right and then sharp left and passes over a cattle-grid. Continue along the track until you reach the motor road again.

Turn left along the road for about 300 yards, passing first a small car park on the left, surrounded by a ring of large stones, then a small layby with room for 4 or 5 cars, again on the left. About 20 yards beyond the far end of this, where the road makes a slight bend to the left, fork half-right off it on a narrow path through the heather. Essentially you are going to head in a straight line towards the high rocks in the distance, so try to keep on the main path and maintain this line, and shortly after passing between two tall rock outcrops you will reach a junction of several paths. Bear slightly right here along the broadest path and soon you will reach the broad access drive: turn right along it for the Information Centre, left to return to the car park.

Brimham Rocks

29. Two Walks from the Embsay and Bolton Abbey Steam Railway

The Embsay and Bolton Abbey Steam Railway runs every Sunday throughout the year and most days during the summer.

Walk a. From Embsay to Embsay Crag.

3½ miles (5¾ km). This walk gives you a real taste of hill-walking, with a steep, but easy climb to a 1200 foot summit with excellent views.

For those coming by car, there is a car-park at the top end of Embsay village near Elm Tree Square and the Elm Tree Inn. To join the walk, pass the Inn and continue along Pasture Road. Embsay Station is well-signposted near the bottom end of the village, and here there are a car-park for rail users, a gift shop and refreshments.

For the walk, return up the station access road, cross straight over the main road and take West Lane opposite. At the next junction keep straight forward, ignoring Dalacres Crescent on the right, and at the T-junction at the top of the hill turn left along Pasture Road. Pass an old mill with its millpond on the left and a fine old hall, the Manor House, with datestones of 1652 and 1665 on the right. After passing Manor Farm on the right, look right to see Embsay Crag, the goal of today's walk. Yes, you really are going up there!

The road crosses Embsay Beck and rises to a junction: keep right. With the embankment of Embsay Reservoir ahead, keep left when the road forks. The signpost says Embsay Crag 1 mile. The road passes to the left of the reservoir car-park and the reservoir, which is used by Craven Sailing Club. The tarmac ends, but the bridleway continues along the walled track. (At the far end of the reservoir a signpost indicates a pleasant permissive path which leads in a clockwise direction round the reservoir back to the reservoir car-park.)

Where the track bends left, cross the stile on the right. An Information Board indicates that we are now entering the Barden Moor Access Area. Follow the track parallel to the wall on the right. This can be wet. Blue topped posts indicate the route of the bridleway, which we shall follow all the way to the summit. When the path forks, keep right on the bridlepath, which after following the reservoir wall for a short distance and crossing a footbridge begins to climb and bears left. The marker posts are a sure guide to our route.

The final part of the climb to the summit is very steep. Behind one at the top is the rolling heather moorland of Barden Moor, the summit rocks of Simon's Seat can be seen, and moving much further round

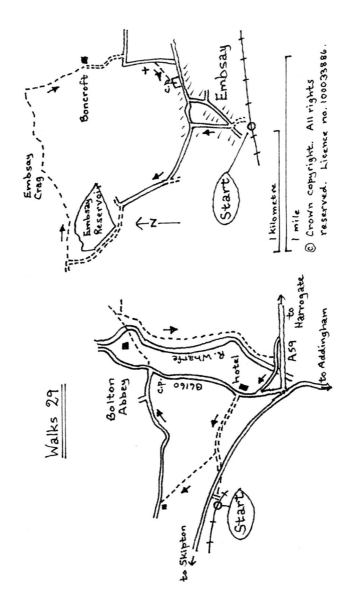

Walks 29

Boncroft

Embsay Crag

Embsay Reservoir

c.p.

Embsay

Start

← N

1 kilometre

1 mile

Bolton Abbey

c.p.

D6160

hotel

R. Wharfe

to Harrogate

A59

to Addingham

to Skipton

Start

Chelker Reservoir with its four wind turbines, then Skipton Moor and Skipton itself down in the dip.

Leave the summit on the opposite side from your arrival, on a clear path which descends over a subsidiary crag towards the intake wall. After a short distance blue topped posts again point the way. Having reached the wall, you pass a stone sheepfold, and 40 yards further on come to a gate in the wall signposted as a footpath and bridleway to Eastby.

Go through the gate and walk down the field parallel to the wall on the right. The whaleback shape of Pendle Hill can be seen in the distance to the right. At one point on the way down cross through the ditch to your right over to the wall. Go through a gate into a walled lane. The wall on the right soon ends, but follow the wall on the left down to Boncroft Farm. On the way down you pass a bench and an information board about Milking Hill Wood. At the farm you join a tarmac road.

Follow it down to the edge of the hamlet of Eastby and turn right along the road. Where it bends left, in the grounds on the right is the large house known as Embsay Kirk; here was the original site of the monastery which was later moved to Bolton Abbey, and the O.S. map still marks a Monk's Well. Pass St. Mary's Church, and 50 yards further, at the entrance to Greenside, go through a stile on the corner and follow the clear path diagonally across the field to the far corner. Look right for a last view of Embsay Crag – yes, you really have been up there! Cross the next stile and follow the enclosed path along. Cross another stile and bear left to a gate into the car-park. Walk through the car-park to the road and turn right, and follow the main road back to the station.

Walk b. From Bolton Abbey Station to Bolton Abbey.

3½ miles (5¾ km). Bolton Abbey Station is signposted off the A59 Harrogate-Skipton road just west of Bolton Abbey. The station buildings are attractive and there are a café and gift shop and a large car-park for users of the railway.

Bolton Abbey, tucked into a bend in the River Wharfe, is one of the beauty spots of the Dales, crowded on summer weekends. The priory (it never was an abbey) for Augustinian Canons was founded in 1151 by Alicia de Romilly of Skipton Castle. It was suppressed by King Henry VIII in 1539. The nave continued in use as a parish church, but the eastern parts fell into ruin. In the 18th century the estate came into the possession of the Dukes of Devonshire, who still own it, and the priory gatehouse was made into a shooting lodge.

Leave the station by the main access road, pass through the wide white gates and immediately turn right past a row of houses. Follow the footpath to the main road (A59), bear right for a few yards then cross the road (care!) to a small gate and bridleway sign opposite. Follow this lane (the old A59) for about 150 yards to a stile on the left, immediately before a wall comes down the field on the left. Cross the stile and bear left up the field towards three trees on the skyline. At the top of the hill look back for the view down Wharfedale to Ilkley.

Cross the high step-stile in the wall between the first and second trees, go through the gate in the fence on the right and bear left over the next field, aiming for the right hand end of the large barns of Hesketh House Farm. There join a track and bear right along it and out onto a road. Turn right and follow this quiet road down to Bolton Abbey village.

Pass the village hall and the post office/gift shop (refreshments) by the large car-park, then continue along the road, keeping left where it forks. More refreshments are available at the Tea Cottage ahead. Cross the main road diagonally left to the hole in the wall opposite, which gives access to the priory and the riverside. Go down the long flight of steps and follow the path to the first gate.

For the priory turn left before the gate – the fine house over to the right is known as the Rectory, which was built in the 15th century as a school – and follow the path to the western entrance to the church. Bolton Hall, the former priory gatehouse, is over to the left. The large western tower of the church was started in 1520 and never completed: note how it does not fit with the beautiful 13th century Early English Gothic portal behind.

For the riverside go through the gate and keep straight on. Make your way to the footbridge over the Wharfe – the stepping stones to the left of it are irregular, slippery, often under water and not to be recommended. Cross the bridge and turn left, but soon take the steps forking right – the riverside beach down to the left is a favourite picnic spot – in a few yards forking right again and climbing the hillside.

Before you reach the top of the hill take the path forking right (signposted Storiths). There is a fine view of the priory and the river. At the fork at the top keep right (signposted Bolton Bridge) on a level path contouring high above the river. Cross a stile and in a few yards a footbridge and walk along the right hand edge of the field. Cross a stile by a large gate on the right and follow the fence on the right along and downhill. Where it turns sharp right, keep straight forward to a stile in the cross fence at the bottom.

Cross the sleeper bridge and walk straight across the large field. The right of way does not cross to the riverside, but heads for a large gate in the fence ahead. From that gate make for the next gate, from which you will see a track climbing the slope ahead: take that. Half right Bolton Bridge, which you are shortly going to cross, is visible. Don't go through the gate at the top, but pass to the right of it and walk along to a stile by the next gate. The river is below. Now follow the fence on the right, down almost to river level, then follow the clear path over the middle of the last field before the farm. Cross the stile on the far side and follow the enclosed path to the road.

Turn right. This is the old A59 again, which you are going to follow all the way back to the start. Cross Bolton Bridge and follow the road to the T-junction. Cross over towards the Abbey Tea Rooms and turn right along the footway. On the other side of the road is the Devonshire Arms Country House Hotel. Where the main road swings right past the hotel, fork left along the continuation of the old road. Follow it all the way to its end at the new road. Cross this and turn right along the footway to follow your outward route back to the station.

Walk 30

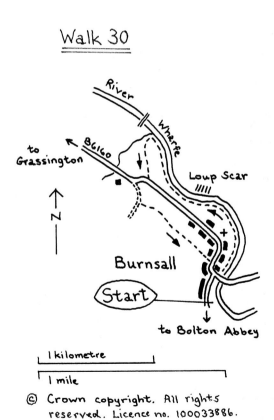

30. Burnsall

2 miles (3¼ km); Explorer OL2. An attractive riverside path with many pleasant picnic spots leads to a bouncy suspension bridge, stepping stones over the river (not recommended when the river is high) and a final chance for a picnic, then for those who enjoy negotiating stiles, there are 11 (none difficult) in quick succession on the return route. Refreshments are available at the Wharfe View Tea Rooms and the Red Lion Hotel. Don't miss a look at the old Grammar School which dates from 1602. The first section of the riverside path as far as two benches is suitable for pushchairs.

By bus: Pride of the Dales No.74 Ilkley-Grassington via Bolton Abbey and Burnsall; Mon-Sat 2-hourly.
By car: Park in Burnsall village.

Walk down to the river by the side of the Red Lion and along the path with the river on the right. The path usually keeps close to the river, but at one point rises above it, with Loup Scar, a limestone cliff, on the other side. Follow the path to the suspension bridge and stepping stones.

Retrace your route through the first gate and over the footbridge. Now bear right up a stepped path, climbing fairly steeply. This path is known locally as "Postman's Steps" and emerges onto the road. Turn right for about 200 yards, taking care on this busy section, then on a slight right hand bend a short distance before some barns go up a farm lane on the left.

Follow the lane to where a stile crosses the wall on the left opposite another on the right (almost underneath the electricity wires). Cross the one on the left (the first of the 11) and head straight up the slope towards the group of trees on the skyline. Before you reach them the path bears slightly right and drops to a stile in the wall ahead. Now bear half right, passing under the power lines, to a stile in the bottom corner of the field. The route is now straight across a number of fields, from one stile to the next, all the way back to Burnsall. As you approach the village the bulk of Burnsall Fell looms large to the right. Finally you pass through a small gate to the left of an electricity sub-station and walk forward to the road. Turn right for the centre of the village.

Record of Walks completed

Date	Walk	Start time	Finish Time	Comments
	1. Roundhay Park and Gorge			
	2. Temple Newsam			
	3. Golden Acre			
	4. Fairburn Ings			
	5. Leeds/Bradford Airport and Rawdon Billing			
	6. The Cow and Calf Rocks, Ilkley			
	7. Shipley Glen			

Date	Walk	Start time	Finish time	Comments
	8. St. Ives			
	9. Haworth and the Worth Valley Railway			
	10. Northcliffe Woods, 'Six Days Only', Heaton Woods			
	11. Anglers Country Park and the Heronry			
	12. Pugneys Country Park and Sandal Castle			
	13. The Yorkshire Sculpture Park			
	14. Hemsworth Water Park and Vale Head Park			
	15. Stanley Marsh Nature Reserve			
	16. Tunnel End and Close Gate Bridge			

Date	Walk	Start time	Finish time	Comments
	17. Digley Reservoir			
	18. Castle Hill			
	19. The Kirklees Light Railway			
	20. The Calder & Hebble Navigation			
	21. Two Reservoir Walks – Short walk			
	21. Two Reservoir Walks – Longer walk			
	22. Heptonstall and the Colden Valley			
	23. Shibden Valley			
	24. Ogden Water			

Date	Walk	Start time	Finish time	Comments
	25. The Great Wall of Todmorden			
	26. Knaresborough: River, Castle and Cave			
	27. Harrogate: Valley Gardens, Pine Woods			
	28. Brimham Rocks			
	29. Embsay Crag			
	29. Bolton Abbey			
	30. Burnsall			